# FUNDAMENTALISM
in
American Religion
1880 - 1950

A forty-five-volume facsimile series
reproducing often extremely rare material
documenting the development of one of the
major religious movements of our time

■ *Edited by*
**Joel A. Carpenter**
Billy Graham Center, Wheaton College
■ *Advisory Editors*
**Donald W. Dayton,**
Northern Baptist Theological Seminary
**George M. Marsden,**
Duke University
**Mark A. Noll,**
Wheaton College
**Grant Wacker,**
University of North Carolina

A GARLAND SERIES

# ■ Conservative Call to Arms

*Edited with an introduction by*
Joel A. Carpenter

*Garland Publishing*
*New York & London 1988*

For a list of the titles in this series, see the final pages of this volume.

Introduction copyright © 1988 by Joel A. Carpenter
All rights reserved

The facsimile of *The Menace of Modernism* has been made from a copy in the Wheaton College Library; that of *What the War Teaches* is from a copy in the Library of Congress.

**Library of Congress Cataloging-in-Publication Data**
Conservative call to arms.

(Fundamentalism in American religion, 1880-1950)
Reprint (1st work). Originally published: New York,
N.Y. : Christian Alliance Pub. Co., 1917.
Reprint (2nd work). Originally published: Los Angeles,
Calif.: Biola Book Room, Bible Institute of Los Angeles,
c1918.
Contents: The menace of modernism / William B. Riley --
What the war teaches, or, the Greatest lessons of
1917 / ReubenA. Torrey.
1. Modernism--Controversial literature. 2. World War,
1914-1918--Religious aspects. I. Carpenter, Joel A.
II. Riley, W. B. (William Bell), 1861-1947. Menace of
modernism. 1988. III. Torrey, R. A. (Reuben Archer),
18546-1928. What the war teaches. IV. Series.
BT82.C66  1988         273'.9         88-4189
ISBN 0-8240-5022-3 (alk. paper)

*Design by Valerie Mergentime*
Printed on acid-free, 250-year-life paper
Manufactured in the United States of America

# CONTENTS

■ *Introduction*

■ *The Menace of Modernism*
    William B. Riley

■ *What the War Teaches, or
The Greatest Lessons of 1917*
    Reuben A. Torrey

# INTRODUCTION

The short book and brief tract reproduced in this volume depict fundamentalism in the process of emerging as a protest movement. These works illustrate how in the years just prior to 1920, a group of conservative evangelicals grew more militant in its response to the liberalization of Protestant theology and the growth of secular trends in the rest of American life. Historical circumstances—such as the secularization of higher education and the war-inflamed anxiety about America's future—were combining with conservative evangelicals' growing sense of having lost cultural influence to mobilize them into an anti-modernist coalition. The years during and just after World War I, then, are an important juncture in the history of fundamentalism.

Indeed, those years mark the final phase of the transition from nineteenth-century reformed evangelicalism to twentieth-century fundamentalism. It is important, as several historians have argued, to resist reading later fundamentalism's threatened, reactionary outlook into earlier conservative evangelicalism.[1] The revivalistic movement which had grown up around Dwight L. Moody (1837–1899), the most influential evangelist in late nineteenth-century America, had a largely positive agenda, not a reactionary one. As late as 1905, one of this movement's leaders, Arthur T. Pierson, described its accomplishments as "Forward Movements."[2] This expansive, fairly hopeful revivalism has been present in fundamentalism, but what made fundamentalists' sense of identity and mission distinct from other evangelical and revivalistic movements, according to historian George Marsden, was its "militant opposition to modernism."[3] So the question of how evangelical revivalists were shaped into militant anti-modernists is one which those who wish to understand fundamentalism need to answer. The works reprinted in this volume provide clear and forceful illustrations of the fundamentalist mentality in the making, of the "remarkable shift from moderation to militancy" which the wartime spirit of 1917–1919 fostered among conservative evangelicals.[4]

*The Menace of Modernism* (New York: Christian Alliance Publications, 1917) was written by William Bell Riley (1861–1947), who was at the time of the book's publication the pastor of the First Baptist Church of Minneapolis and the president of the Northwestern Bible and Missionary Training School. A Kentucky-bred graduate of Hanover College in Indiana and the Southern Baptist Theological Seminary in Louisville, Riley was a prominent pastor and an unctuous evangelist. He also had become a leader in the "prophetic Bible conference" movement, which promoted a millenarian view of Christ's Second Coming and the church's mission. By 1917, Riley was on the verge of becoming the chief organizer and public spokesperson for the fundamentalist movement. When the fundamentalist-modernist conflict erupted in the 1920s Riley's star rose; he became the president of the World Christian Fundamentals Association and publisher of the WCFA organ, *Christian Fundamentals in School and Church,* the director of the Anti-Evolution League of Minnesota, and the regional "warlord" of the fundamentalist forces in Minnesota and neighboring states.[5]

*The Menace of Modernism* shows Riley's growing conviction that "modernism" (theological liberalism and/or secular humanism), was not just a passing intellectual fashion but a persuasion which held substantial cultural power, particularly in the realm of higher education and among the educated classes. Modernism was a menace, Riley insisted, because it attacked the authority of the Bible, which he took to be the moral foundation for American culture. A whole generation of educated Americans, he feared, was on the verge of stumbling into an abyss of moral suicide because of the modernists' subversion of biblical authority. So, Riley believed, there was a major crisis afoot, and conservatives should rally 'round their colors and "earnestly contend for the faith once delivered to the saints" (Jude 3).

Readers will be interested to note how intensely Riley felt this conflict on a personal level, especially as it reflected the flagging cultural and religious influence of conservative evangelical preachers such as himself. Indeed, this book suggests that populist commitments and emotions were an important facet of the fundamentalist protest. Modernism, as an accomodation of Christian theology to modern secular thought, prompted modernists to attach themselves to the social and educational elites. At a time when educators and scientists in particular were gaining prestige as cultural authorities, Riley relates with great bitterness the friendly relations between modernist ministers (whom, he alleged, were failures in the parish) and the "skeptical" professors of the University of Minnesota (pp. 90–100). And in this "science-mad" age, he complained, professors were looked up to as authorities on all sorts of subjects—even religion—at the expense of pastors, especially those of conservative stripe (pps. 79–81, 87–90, 95, 118 [quote]). Riley's testimony seems to verify the argument that there was a conflict of cultural authority in these years, that traditional and democratic cultural leaders were losing influence to the "experts," the beneficiaries of the revolution in higher education.⁶ Readers will have the opportunity, then, to assess historian R. Laurence Moore's argument that fundamentalism was more a "response to diminished intellectual prestige" than a "response to declining . . . economic status."⁷

At any rate, *The Menace of Modernism* concludes with a call to action. Riley pleaded for a "confederacy" of conservative evangelicals (whom he called "radical conservatives" [pp. 87, 163]) who will add their voice to debates over religion and public policy, and thus in at least some vocal and symbolic ways, counteract the "menace of modernism." He hinted that preliminary talks for such a coalition have begun, and that it might engage in some real power struggles to achieve its goals, such as attempting some purges of schools and denominations (pp. 177–78). At this point, Riley's agenda for action is not clearly stated. He was only months away, however, from founding his anti-modernist magazine, *School and Church,* in 1918, and the World's Christian Fundamentals Association in 1919. So *The Menace of Modernism* is an important waymark in the development of Riley's views, and through his leadership, those of the fundamentalist movement. Its message is an enduring one, as fundamentalists' recent forays against "secular humanism" in American public life make clear.

Riley's book appears to have been produced before American intervention in World War I, or at least before America's anti-German emotions reached fever pitch. But Reuben A. Torrey's short tract, *What the War Teaches, or The Greatest Lessons of 1917* (Los Angeles: BIOLA Book Room, 1918), makes explicit connections between modernism in America and its alleged roots in German philosophy, theology, and biblical criticism. This polemic is a dramatic illustration of the way the war-induced spirit of crisis intensified the belief of conservative evangelical millenarians that they were living in times of unprecedented spiritual and cultural conflict.

The author of *What the War Teaches,* Reuben A. Torrey (1856–1928), was one of the aging "war horses" of conservative evangelicalism. Probably the best-educated of fundamentalism's founders, Torrey was trained for the Congregational ministry at Yale College and Yale Divinity School; and he spent a year of postgraduate study in theology at the universities of Leipzig and Erlangen. In contrast to Riley and most of the other leaders of the emerging fundamentalist coalition, Torrey had read considerably in the literature of German philosophy, biblical criticism, and liberal theology.

Early in his career, however, Torrey made a deliberate choice for traditional orthodoxy, urban evangelism, and popular religious teaching, rather than the mildly liberal theology, comfortable parish ministry, and genteel literary culture to which many well-educated young pastors aspired. Torrey accepted a call to a struggling mission in Minneapolis, became an understudy of Dwight L. Moody, and emerged after 1900 as an urban evangelist of considerable fame, holding campaigns in American, Australian, and British cities. Torrey's forty-five books and nearly two dozen pamphlets were not for the most part learned treatises, but popularly styled works for pastors and laity on the Second Coming, the Holy Spirit and personal piety, the Bible's inerrancy, and evangelism. As such, Torrey's publications complemented his work as a pioneering dean at the Moody Bible Institute of Chicago, and later at the Bible Institute of Los Angeles; his labors as an evangelist; and his lectures on the Bible conference circuit.[8] *What the War Teaches* reflects these commitments, concerns, and experiences. It is a tract for popular consumption on a topic of immediate concern to conservative evangelicals, but it betrays a more-than-passing acquaintance with the works of German philosophers and theologians.

Torrey was only five years older than Riley, but by the eve of the fundamentalist-modernist conflict he had already endured a very strenuous career as an itinerant evangelist and Bible teacher. He apparently lacked the energy and ambition to carry out a major role in the fundamentalist campaigns. Torrey did edit the last two volumes of *The Fundamentals,* write a half dozen polemical treatises in defense of fundamentalist doctrine, and contribute an occasional speech or article to the cause. Yet he was not willing to lead the charge. Torrey had seen the peak of his career already, and appeared to be satisfied with the role of "elder statesman" while more ambitious and energetic lieutenants like Riley emerged to take the lead. Fundamentalism thus was put in the hands of younger, less well-educated, and less articulate leaders. The old guard of the millenarian, Bible School movement of conservative evangelicals was passing, and their decision to "go popular" in their ministry commitments was having an unfortunate consequence. While their movement was richly endowed with popular support and practical training, it was poorly equipped to reproduce intellectually alert leaders.

It would be a misjudgement, however, to suggest that Torrey was a half-hearted fundamentalist. *What the War Teaches* is a trumpet call to action in "the most momentous [year] that any man living has ever seen" (p. 2), and a summons to get busy before "'the night cometh, when no man can work'" (John 9:4).

What did the war "teach" the emerging fundamentalist movement? It confirmed their pessimistic cultural outlook and gave them some ammunition against the modernists. First, wrote Torrey, the war teaches that the Bible is true, for it shows evidence of fulfilled prophecy. It confirms premillennialists' view that the

Jews will hold center stage in the last days of human history, for the capture of Jerusalem and the Balfour Declaration paved the way for the fulfillment of premillennialists' prediction that the Jews will be restored to their homeland. The war also confirms biblical prophecy, Torrey argued, because it gives credence to the prediction of increasing "wars and rumors of wars" and people's "hearts failing them for fear" in the last days. Jesus is coming soon; the events of the past year prove it (pp. 2–6, 14–15).

Another "lesson of 1917," Torrey claimed, is that the horrors of modern warfare confirm the Bible's teaching on human nature and destiny. Contrary to the roseate visions of liberal theologians and progressive humanists, modern science and technology are not moving us towards a new golden age; Western democracies are using their vaunted knowledge to slaughter each other's citizens. The only hope for the human race is in Christ's redemption and his eventual restoration of all things (pp. 8, 12–14).

Torrey leveled his biggest guns at what he saw as the major cause of the war. He argued that the world is suffering from the spiritual and moral demise of its most intellectually and technologically advanced nation, Germany. Germany's descent into barbarity and militarism, he claimed (following closely the recent Allied propaganda), can be attributed to two intellectual trends: the rationalistic religious skepticism of German scholars and their embrace of evolutionary, materialistic philosophy. The result, he argued, has been the decay of Germany's biblically-based morality and her embrace of a generation of philosophers who have glorified war as a major tool of human evolution (pp. 9–11).

Torrey then brought the lesson home: American educators and liberal theologians have embraced these same ideas, and our nation's future forebodes the same universities, colleges, and high schools" (p. 10). Furthermore, he accused theological seminaries of teaching the same "Destructive Criticism, destructive in more senses than one," that opened Germany to brutal and godless philosophies. Americans were fools, he warned, if they would not learn from Germany's sad example (p. 11).

Torrey laid out no explicit program, nor did he call for a new conservative coalition. He simply asked that his readers work with new urgency, for soon "the night cometh," and the church's time to work will soon be over. But he showed very clearly the volatile combination of prophetic expectation and cultural peril which produced fighting fundamentalism. And he named the "two fronts," as Marsden puts it, of the fundamentalists' offensive: against "modernism" in the denominations and against "evolutionism" in the schools. Like *The Menace of Modernism, What the War Teaches* is a classic example of the fundamentalist cultural critique and public agenda. Its themes endure today—in only slightly altered forms.

Joel A. Carpenter
Institute for the Study of American Evangelicals
Wheaton College

## NOTES

1. See especially George M. Marsden, *Fundamentalism and American Culture: The Shaping of Twentieth Century Evangelicalism, 1870–1925* (New York: Oxford University Press, 1980); and Grant Wacker, "The Holy Spirit and the Spirit of the Age in American Protestantism," *Journal of American History* 72 (June 1985): 45–62.

2. Arthur Tappan Pierson, *Forward Movements of the Last Half Century* (New York: Funk and Wagnalls, 1905).

3. Marsden, *Fundamentalism*, 4.

4. *Ibid.,* 141.

5. These details of Riley's career are ably documented in C. Allyn Russell, *Voices of American Fundamentalism: Seven Biographical Studies* (Philadelphia: Westminster, 1976), chapter four, "William Bell Riley: Organizational Fundamentalist" 81–106 (and notes on 237–244); Ferenc Morton Szasz, "Three Fundamentalist Leaders: The Roles of William Bell Riley, John Roach Straton, and William Jennings Bryan in the Fundamentalist-Modernist Controversy" (Ph.D. dissertation, University of Rochester, 1969); and William Vance Trollinger, "One Response to Modernity: Northwestern Bible School and the Fundamentalist Empire of William Bell Riley" (Ph.D dissertation, University of Wisconsin, 1984), chapter I: "The Leader," 19–59.

6. Robert Wiebe, *The Search for Order: 1877–1920* (New York: Hill and Wang, 1966); Burton J. Bledstein, *The Culture of Professionalism: The Middle Class and the Development of Higher Education in America* (New York: W.W. Norton, 1976).

7. R. Lawrence Moore, *Religious Outsiders and the Making of Americans* (New York: Oxford University Press, 1986), 172.

8. Torrey has not yet been treated in a scholarly, analytic biography. Roger Martin, *R. A. Torrey, Apostle of Certainty* (Murfreesboro, Tenn.: Sword of the Lord, 1976), is carefully documented and thorough, but lacks critical detachment. Torrey receives brief but perceptive treatment in William G. McLoughlin, *Modern Revivalism: Charles Grandison Finney to Billy Graham* (New York: Ronald Press, 1959), 366–377. These two works are the sources for biographical details in this paragraph and the preceding one.

# The Menace of Modernism

by

**William B. Riley, D. D.**

Pastor of First Baptist Church, and Superintendent
of Northwestern Bible Training School, Minneapolis.

Christian Alliance Publishing Company
692 Eighth Avenue, New York, N. Y.

COPYRIGHTED 1917.
CHRISTIAN ALLIANCE PUBLISHING COMPANY
692 EIGHTH AVENUE,
NEW YORK.

# CONTENTS.

| Chapter | | Page |
|---|---|---|
| | Foreword | 5 |
| I. | What is the True Meaning of Modernism? | 7 |
| II. | Is Modernism a Real Menace? | 32 |
| III. | Is Modernism Undermining the Evangelical Ministry? | 54 |
| IV. | Has the State University Become a Hot-Bed of Heterodoxy? | 76 |
| V. | Do Our Denominational Colleges Deny the Evangelical Faith? | 105 |
| VI. | Is the Modern Bible School God's Antidote to Skepticism? | 130 |
| VII. | Is a Confederacy of Conservatives the Call of the Hour? | 154 |

### Foreword.

The relation of creed to conduct is argued alike by Reason and Revelation. The Bible says "As a man thinketh in his heart so is he;" and the keenest observers upon human life have been compelled to concede the scientific accuracy of that claim. The faith of today will determine alike the conduct and character of tomorrow. A false theology eventually fruits in foul living.

The opinion of the preacher and the school professor, voiced in the presence of youth, is more than a mere matter of polemics; it is practically a matter of morals, hence the title of this book "The Menace of Modernism." Hundreds of grateful students have already bourne testimony to the help received from the original delivery of this series; the author sends it forth asking no greater reward or return than that of lending similar help to thousands.

## CHAPTER I.

## WHAT IS THE TRUE MEANING OF MODERNISM?

"God, who at sundry times and in divers manners spake in time past unto the fathers by the prophets, hath in these last days spoken unto us by his Son, whom he hath appointed heir of all things, by whom also he made the worlds" (Hebrews 1:1-2).

Theologically, the times are out of joint! The air is filled with speculations and interrogations. A great German professor entitles his book "What is Christianity?" A widely known American discusses "Can I know God, the Father?" A Scotchman contributes a volume on "Can the Old Faith Live with the New?" and a notable Russian devotes his book to the question "What is Religion?" Hastings' "Bible Dictionary" is a series of interrogation points. They stand up so erectly and so regularly that one is reminded not so much of an army on the march as of a halted brigade.

We are now told "in religion nothing is settled!" Every claim must be investigated; every prophet is on trial; every apostle has been ordered into the presence of the Scribes, and even the Master Himself is in Pilate's hall. With the old question "What is Truth?" they are alike confronted, and the answer of each and all must come into the crucible of *"modern thinking."*

The natural result is unrest. This is shared by many who know little on the subject, but whose spiritual nerves are disturbed by the theological storm. The law "like begets like" finds no exception when it comes to a question. One question can create another; and, as the lungs of youth take in more air than those of the aged, so the young men and the young women of the land are breathing the air of skepticism more deeply than is possible to those of mature years, and are correspondingly affected. Henry Drummond once affirmed that many of the finest young men he knew in the Universities of the Old World were sorely disturbed over the whole question of Christianity; and were doubters, not because they desired to be, but because no man had appeared whose philosophy of religion had met their mental demands.

To help young men and women when they are passing through the critical hours of religious thought and experience is the acme of privilege. Such a work is more nearly infinite in its final reach than any other possible to

# Meaning of Modernism?

the human teacher. Impelled by that motive, I speak on "The True Meaning of Modernism."

In order, therefore, to get a proper setting, both for our theme and the proper interpretation of the text quoted, permit me, first of all, to present

### The Old Conception.

Our text speaks of both the old and the new.

"God, who at sundry times and in diverse manners spake in time past unto the fathers by the prophets."

There are at least three features of the old conception, each of which has now passed away. They are, first, that the Bible was finished in heaven and handed down; second, that the King James Version was absolutely inerrant; third, that its literal acceptance and interpretation was, alone, correct.

*Was the Bible finished in heaven and handed down?*

That is the charge that is made against the old conception, and perhaps there have been people in the world who thought it. A notable representative of Modernism claims to have had a fellow seminary student who thought that way. He says: "My friend was brought up on a western farm. He had spent a goodly portion of his life in hoeing corn. While hoeing corn a certain conception of the Bible had crystallized in his mind which he supposed to be very true, and which was similar to the conception of Joseph Smith regarding the book of Mormon. He (Joseph) believed that the Bible was found already written and preserved in a sacred book. The leaves of the book were plates of gold, bound together with three gold rings, and on the top of the book there was a pair of supernatural spectacles by means of which it was possible for him to interpret the mysterious language in which the divine book was written.

"Our farmer believed the Bible had been written in heaven and bound in heaven, and dropped down in some mysterious way upon the earth." And then the same writer goes the length of saying: "Most young men come to schools of theology with the pagan conception that the divine Book came down out of heaven much as the Koran is said to have done in the legend. We once read a learned article on 'Our English Bible, Where Did We

Get It?' in which the author said some of the Jewish Rabbis held to the opinion that the entire Old Testament, as we have it in the Hebrew, was not produced on the earth at all, but was made in heaven. The angels up there, or some other power, assisted, of course, by inspiration, made the volume, book by book, and thus handed it down to mortals here below."

We do not know the age of our friend—this exponent of Modernism. It may be that he went to school with one of these fellows. When I was in college, 1881-1885, I never met a man who held that old conception; and when in the theological seminary, 1885-1888, I met no such man, though my seminary *was* one of the largest on this continent and a majority of its attendants were farm-bred. In the active pastorate, since that time, I have never met an intelligent man who contended for such a position; consequently I conclude that that part of the old conception has now passed.

*Is the King James version absolutely inerrant?*

On this point we are inclined to think that, even unto comparatively recent years, such a theory has been entertained. The result, of course, is to make a sort of fetish of the book. That is why, in many a family, it is kept on the center-table and seldom used. They do not want to soil its sacredness. Dr. Arthur T. Pierson tells the story of a Karen village into which a travelling Mussulman had come bearing a mysterious book, which he told the Karens was sacred and entitled to divine honors. It was accepted, and wrapped in muslin and encased in a basket work of reeds, like Moses' cradle. The mysterious book became deified and venerated, a kind of high priest and sacristan combined. When Boardman came to the village he was asked by the Karens to examine it, and it was found to be the "Book of Common Prayer and Psalms," an Oxford edition in English, and Mr. Boardman, with joy, entered upon its exposition, and like Paul at Athens, declared unto them the true God. And even now in more remote districts, where educational advantages have been few, the history of the Bible is unknown. Of its translation from language to language they have never learned, and yet I think it would be accepted without fear of successful controversy that such fogies in Biblical knowledge are few, and their funerals are nigh at hand.

To be sure, there are multitudes who do not understand that the Scriptures were originally written either in Hebrew, Aramaic or Greek; that all the original versions were lost, and that the copies of the New Testament date many years this side of Jesus, and that our Scriptures are translations which have come by the way of the Septuagint and Coptic versions, and have been improved in the passage by Martin Luther, John Wycliffe, Tyndale, Covedale, and others; that in 1611, seventy of the most scholarly men, at the King's command, gave us our "authorized version," and that between 1870 and 1885 the Canterbury Revision Committee, made up of a hundred of the world's most accurate scholars, accomplished the text of the Revised Version. To claim, therefore, inerrancy for the King James Version, or even for the Revised Version, is to claim inerrancy for men who never professed it for themselves; to clothe with the claim of verbal inspiration a company of men who would almost quit their graves to repudiate such equality with prophet and apostle.

*Is a literal acceptance and interpretation alone correct?*

This doctrine has always had its adherents,

and perhaps always will. Yet it belongs distinctly to the old conception.

Out of this view has grown the very claim with which modern science has been compelled to take issue. It was this view that made men say that God created the earth in six *"literal"* days of twenty-four hours each. It was this view that led men to believe that the earth was stationary and the heavenly bodies revolved around it; and, in consequence, gave easy consent to the theory that at Joshua's command, the sun stood still. It was this conception that gave rise to John Jasper's famous sermon on "The Sun Do Move." It was this conception that led even so remarkable a man as John Calvin to oppose Copernicus by an appeal to the Ninety-third Psalm: "The world also is stablished, that it cannot be moved." But John Calvin has been dead a good long while, and as for John Jasper, his earnestness and eloquence may be accepted as a perfect atonement for his ignorance: and the part he played in theological thinking ought never to be deplored by men who imagine themselves to be intelligent. The greatest and grandest of truths may be discredited by unwarranted advocacy and undue emphasis.

## The New Conception.

Permit me to remark that in discussing this phase of our theme I do not refer as yet to the second part of our text, for I am not fully persuaded that the new conception is based upon the revelation of Christ; that relates itself, rather, to another thought yet to be developed, namely, the true conception.

But the new conception has some definite characterizations, each one of which has emanated from what is proudly called "the modern mind." They also might be stated under three heads.

First: The Bible is purely human in its origin and authorship; second, the inspiration of the Bible exists only in its ability to inspire, and finally, its interpretation is a matter of mental convenience.

To prove that I do no injustice in these definitions of the new conception, let me appeal to a man who is proudly accepted as a leader among new theologians. Dr. Charles Edward Jefferson has a volume entitled "Things Fundamental" of which "The Outlook"—the mouth-piece of Modernism—says: "In point of culture, breadth, and spiritual power, Dr. Jefferson's discourses rank among the best utterances of the pulpit." Concerning it, "The Churchman" also remarks: "Thoroughly excellent! Should be read widely." "The Congregationalist" also declares: "In this series of sermons Dr. Jefferson has thought his subjects through until they have a crystal clearness in his mind before he utters them in speech. The discussions are eminently sane."

So then, the new conception is, first of all, that—

*The Bible is purely human in its origin and authorship.*

I appeal to Dr. Jefferson. He says: "The modern conception makes the Bible human. Because this is a human book it is going to be studied, by and by, in all seminaries and colleges. When men learn that it was not dictated, but that it came up out of the human heart, they want to know it." We call attention particularly to the latter phrase: "When men learn that it was not dictated, but that it *came up out of the human heart* they will want to know it."

He continues: "The new scholarship makes it clear that the Bible was not produced instantaneously. Like all things else which have ever been upon this earth, it grew. Through at least fifteen hundred years it kept on growing. And in it, therefore, we have the advancing stages of an unfolding life. A particular race, beginning near the bottom, climbs little by little in the face of tremendous obstacles from the darkness of barbarism into a glorious light. Now in all growing life there must be that which is immature, crude, mistaken. If a race grows as a man does, there must be, first childhood and then youth. What a race does and thinks as a child, it will cease to think and do when it becomes a man, for a race like a man puts away childish things. If you are ever tempted, therefore, to make sport of the crudities of the Old Testament, bear in mind that without these crudities the fuller life would have been impossible. We are living in a scientific age when men are intensely interested in origins. Why should you push the Old Testament away with scorn when it contains the story of the origins of our religion? A book is not to be despised simply because *parts of it have been outgrown.*"

The new conception is responsible for the idea that *inspiration exists only in its ability to inspire.* The same writer asks the question "Is the Bible inspired?" and answers "It is." "How do you know?" Answer—"Because it inspires?" That he does not mean what our fathers meant by inspiration is perfectly evident when he says: "Modern scholarship has compelled us to give up the doctrine of verbal inspiration. According to that theory, the Bible is inerrant. It is an infallible book." This theory of infallibility, he declares, the modern conception believes "no longer tenable." And then he boldly asserts: "The Bible contains error. There are errors in the text. The text in many places is undoubtedly corrupt. There are errors in translation. The Jewish historians occasionally slipped. The conceptions of the physical universe held by the men who wrote the Scriptures are not the conceptions which we know to be true. It is not wise, therefore, to use the word 'infallible.' . . . It is not infallible in its arguments, for some of its arguments are weak. It is not infallible in its moral sanctions, for the Hebrews undoubtedly sometimes confounded their own impulses with the voice of God. It is not infallible in the expectations of even its greatest men, for all the apostles expected Jesus to return within their own lifetime. In what sense, then, is the Bible an infallible book? If a man earn-

## Meaning of Modernism? 19

estly wants to find his way to God, the Bible will surely help him find that way. In that sense, and in that sense only, have we any right to say the Bible is infallible."

Again this recognized leader among the modern thinkers makes the interpretation of the Bible *a matter of mental and personal convenience.* When he comes upon a statement in Scripture that seems to be in conflict with science, such as Joshua's command of the sun to stand still, he calls it "poetry." When he comes upon a prophecy in Daniel in which he does not believe he says: "Daniel was mistaken." When he comes to the book of Job he declares it "fiction." The book of Jonah goes into the same category. The creation of Eve "is a myth." When he comes to the question of authorship, is it of God or man, he says, "It is of man." In answer to the question, "Is it right to say that God wrote the Bible" he says, "No, He did not write it. Every page of the Bible is written by man. The lights and shadows of his moods, the depression and rapture of his spirit play over its pages. Its contents came up out of the cavernous depths of the human heart. The light that lights every man that comes into the world came up out of the heart."

When he comes to the doctrine of the imminent coming of Christ he dubs it "an apostle's mistake." Then he concludes by saying that "the Bible is a useful book. It was written by honest men. It does not deceive." He declares that in comparison with the so-called sacred books of the East it is a vast improvement; and while denying to its authors any exclusive experience of inspiration, he yet affirms of the Jews, through whom it came, "No other tribe ever took God in as did the Hebrew people" and makes the poetic remark that there "have been isolated mountain peaks in Asia, but there is a veritable mountain range that culminates in Jesus of Nazareth."

Let me repeat, therefore, for the sake of emphasis, that the new conception of Christianity stands for the assertions that the Bible is purely of human origin and authorship: that its inspiration exists only in its ability to inspire: and that its interpretation is a matter of convenience.

From this I turn to the teaching of the text, which to me, is

### The True Conception.

"God, who at sundry times and in diverse manners spake in time past, unto the fathers by the prophets, hath in these last days spoken unto us by his Son, whom he hath appointed heir of all things; by whom also he made the worlds."

What Paul teaches in this epistle to the Hebrews is this:

*The Bible is divine in origin, and human in expression.*

In the truest sense God is its author. He is the One who "spake in time past, unto the fathers by the prophets." That is the universal claim of the Old Testament authors. Moses repudiated the idea that the five books of the Pentateuch were his thoughts, his feelings and his expression. Again and again he affirmed the Divine authorship.

When I was a lad, the girls in the country where I grew up used to have a custom of making a wish covering something that their souls ardently desired, and then opening the Bible at random; if their eyes rested on the words "and it came to pass," that was accepted as a promise that the heart's desire was to be granted. But that phrase "and it came to pass" is no more a recurrent one in the Scriptures than the other, "The Lord spake unto me, saying . . . " Pick up your Bible and test out what I am declaring.

In the preparation of this discourse I opened my Bible at random, except that I struck into its early part, knowing that I would be in one of the five books of Moses. The place was the fourth chapter of Leviticus. The first sentence of it was this, "The Lord spake unto Moses, saying," etc. Every word of that chapter is claimed as the word, not of Moses, but of the Lord. Absolutely the same thing is true of the fifth chapter, and lest men should forget, before he finishes the fifth chapter, Moses introduces it into the fourteenth verse, saying, "And the Lord spake unto me." The sixth chapter is opened after the same manner; in the eighth verse it is repeated; in the nineteenth it occurs, and yet again in the twenty-fourth, and so on.

Not scores, but hundreds of times is this claim made in the Old Testament. It is in perfect line with the claims of inspiration presented in the New. The attitude of the new conception as advanced by the so-called liberal ministers of the day, viz.—"The Bible was not dictated, but came up out of the human heart," is opposed by the apostle John when he begins the greatest book in the Bible —the Revelation—with the statement, "The Revelation of Jesus Christ, which came unto him to show unto his servant the things which must shortly come to pass. And he sent and signified it by his angel unto his servant John." As between Dr. Jefferson and the apostle John, I find little difficulty of choice.

Dr. B. H. Carroll, easily one of the most scholarly men of his day, and a man whose logic was relentless, says: "In the days of my infidelity I never doubted the Scripture claim of inspiration. . . . The trifling expedient of accepting the Bible as 'inspired in spots' never occurred to me. To accept with Renan, its natural parts and arbitrarily deny its supernatural, or to accept with some the book as from God, and then strike at its heart by a false interpretation that denied the the divinity and vicarious expiation of Jesus—these were follies of which I was never guilty, follies for which, even yet, I have never seen or heard a respectable excuse. To me it was always 'Aut Cæsar, aut nihil'—(either Cæsar or nothing). What anybody wanted, in a religious way, with the shell after the kernel was gone, I never could understand."

The New Theology in its discrediting of the divine origin of Scripture and the historical standing of the separate books that make it up, is not faring well even at the hands of its own friends. A recent writer calls our attention to the fact that not long since Harnack disturbed his own company by arguing with great ability that Luke—the physician—was the author of both the Gospel and the Acts. Dr. William Ramsay in his changed attitude, became a strong advocate of the historicity of the Acts. James Drummond, the great Unitarian scholar of Manchester, and William Sanday, of the Christ Church, Oxford, have alike championed the Johannine authorship of the fourth Gospel; and even accept the genuineness of 1st and 2nd Peter. James is defended by Mayer; and the Apocalypse, which has held a horror for every higher critic, is declared to be from the pen of John, by Swets of Cambridge.

To quote the language of Uncle Remus "Truth ain't never been hurt yit by folks not believin' it." Or, if one wants good English, let Dr. Jefferson himself speak his saner thought, "For fourteen hundred years the sun was misinterpreted. It made no difference to the sun. Ptolemy had a wrong conception, but the sun kept right on shining. He flooded every day with light, and went out into the fields every summer and aided the farmers in

## Meaning of Modernism? 25

bringing in their crops."

The Bible has not retired from its soul-illuminating and soul-saving work because skeptics have said it was only of human origin. As men come to study it more, its effulgence increases, and it is no longer "a lamp to their feet, and a light to their pathway" only, but it is the central sun before the rays of which the night of ignorance and unbelief is paling, and in the light of which men, who have eyes to see, walk with certain and steady tread.

The true conception also is to the effect that *the accepted versions of the Bible are all substantially correct.* I do not wonder that many a young man, sitting in the modern theological seminary, is staggered in his faith and brought to believe that the Bible is not worth retention, if what Dr. Jefferson says is true. He declares that the young man who comes into the school of theology today, with his pagan conception of the Bible as a divine book, is told that "there are 150,000 variations in the text of the New Testament." That is enough to stagger any man!

It is so big a lie that it ought to stagger the professor who tells it more than the student who hears it. It reminds one of Sandy, the

Scotch preacher. He was given to exaggeration, and one of his elders had taken him to task about it. They affected a covenant, and the deacon was to whistle every time Sandy became excited and over-enthusiastic. The very next time he came into the pulpit he waxed eloquent, and finally said, "You remember when Samson caught the 300,000 foxes, and tying the firebrands to their tails, turned them loose into the corn." Thereupon the Deacon whistled! "Oh, I mean 30,000 foxes" said Sandy; upon which the Deacon whistled again; but Sandy replied, "You can blow your blarsted horn as often as you like; I'll not take another fox's tail off."

The Modern theologian is far more accommodating than was the old Scotchman. He is ready, when cornered, to come down. And now we have the delightful privilege of telling you that the same man who says that the theological student must face the fact that there are 150,000 variations in the text of the New Testament, "gets down" until he agrees with the ultra-conservatives. I quote from his book lest men might doubt it: "I suppose there are people who think that as a result of all the discoveries made by recent scholarship

## Meaning of Modernism? 27

the Bible has been amended, expurgated. Such persons are mistaken. Our King James version dates from the beginning of the seventeenth century. About twenty-five years ago a new version was made. Many of the greatest scholars of the world were engaged in this revision. But when they had completed their work, the old Book was practically unchanged. Not one book was dropped out of the big volume. If, any one alarmed, thinking that possibly one of the books has escaped, should plunge into this book, he would hear a cheery voice saying what Paul said to the Philippian jailer, 'Do thyself no harm, we are all here!' Not a chapter was dropped out from the Old Testament or the New. Not a verse was expunged which affects any cardinal doctrine of the Christian religion. A few verses here and there were removed, because there were good reasons for thinking that these verses had slipped into the body of the text from the margin of some ancient manuscript. But generally speaking, the Bible today is just what it was in the days of the Reformation." The ultra-conservative could ask no greater concession! In that speech Modernism is vanquished by moral honesty!

Wescott and Hort, whose scholarship even a Jefferson will not question, affirm that so far as the New Testament is concerned, that of the translations that have occurred in 1500 years there is not an essential change in one word out of a thousand. Once more I repeat it with all the vigor of my soul, "the accepted versions of the Bible are all substantially correct."

*The true interpretation of the Bible involves both the literal and the spiritual.*

Paul's statement of truth finds a thousand illustrations in the Scriptures: "That is not first which is spiritual, but that which is natural, and afterwards that which is spiritual." The first application to be made of the Scriptural assertion is the natural and the literal, and the second is the spiritual; in fact, the symbolical.

Spiritual truth must be spiritually interpreted. The man who has no experience of it can, in the nature of the case, have little knowledge of it. "The natural man receiveth not the things of the Spirit, they are foolishness unto him, neither indeed can he know them because they are spiritually discerned." It is no marvel that many otherwise learned men find the Bible an enigma and stumble alike at literalism and symbolism. The spiritual life is essential to a spiritual understanding. Truly there is "a witness of the Spirit of God." As Ward Beecher says, "A moral intelligence is not infallible but comes nearer to infallibility than the lower reason! It is impossible without holiness to see God, and without willingness to submit to His way no man will clearly perceive what He says."

When Saul was stricken on the way to Damascus, there was a voice from heaven; but the clear word was only as the sound of thunder to his unconverted and unregenerate attendants. "If any man is willing to do God's will he shall know of the teaching whether it be from God." It may sound like a severe arraignment of the modern man who denies the deity of Christ and decries the authority of the Word, to be classed with those ancients who did the same, since he imagines that by the law of evolution, he is a great improvement; and yet, we are fully persuaded that Paul's language to the Corinthians is the adequate explanation of the attitude of many of those who boast the wisdom of this world: "We preach Christ, unto the Jews a stumbling block, and unto the Greeks foolishness, but unto them which are called, both Jews and Greeks, Christ the power of God, and the wisdom of God."

This last sentence leads us to our last remark on the true conception!

It involves the fact that *to the sincere believer the Bible is a book of both light and life.* I know the ease with which young men are moved by an appeal to the eminently great. Horace Bushnell is not to be despised in the world of scholars, and Horace Bushnell says: "The worldly spirit shuts the Bible: the Spirit of God makes it a fire, flaming out all meaning and glorious truth." Richard Cecil, speaking of the Bible, says: "Either study it as removing some obstructions that keep God and thee asunder, or as supplying some uniting power to bring God and thee together;" while John Quincy Adams declared, "The first and almost the only book deserving universal attention is the Bible. It is a book which neither the ignorant and weakest, nor the most learned and intelligent mind can read without improvement." Judged by its fruits, new theology, another name for Modernism, has no defense for its existence; while conservatism has given to the world its Christianity, and to Christ His Church.

## CHAPTER II.

## IS MODERNISM A REAL MENACE?
### II John 1:7-11.

Sermon preached in the First Baptist Church, Minneapolis, May 21, 1916. Occasion: Convention Sunday of the Northern Baptists.

If it be true that "since the days of Kant in philosophy and Darwin in science we have lived in a world of thought peopled with new intellectual citizens" as the author of "The Church and the Changing Order" contends, one need not be surprised to find the thinking of the century rather confused, since these gentlemen, approaching kindred themes from the separate standpoints of philosophy and science, came to exactly opposite conclusions; Kant, contending that in the trial of life the strongest and best equipped will finally fail, while Darwin insists that the result will be "the survival of the fittest,"—conclusions which really gave occasion to Schopenhauer's dictum, "We are all fools living in a fool world." When one gives himself to a study of that so-called "modernism," which is supposed to have originated with these men, he is compelled to consent that Schopenhauer had much basis for his remark. Paradoxical as it may sound, John, writing twenty centuries ago, was dealing with this exact propaganda, and we should give candid consideration to what he has to say:

"For many deceivers are entered into the world, who confess not that Jesus Christ is come in the flesh. This is a deceiver and an antichrist. Look to yourselves, that we lose not those things which we have wrought, but that we receive a full reward. Whosoever transgresseth, and abideth not in the doctrine of Christ, hath not God. He that abideth in the doctrine of Christ, he hath both the Father and the Son. If there come any unto you, and bring not this doctrine, receive him not into your house; neither bid him Godsped: for he that biddeth him Godspeed is partaker of his evil deeds" (II Jno. 1:7-11).

Describing their theology, he denominates its representatives as apostles of deception, and brings against their propaganda the indictment of infidelity, declaring that all who participate with them are, alike, members of the Antichrist. Is he justified in this somewhat rabid arraignment?

### The Apostles of Deception.

He describes them after this manner:

"Many deceivers have gone out into the world, who confess not that Jesus Christ is coming in the flesh. This is a deceiver and an antichrist." Careful study of the language used brings out three suggestions.

*These were nominal Disciples.*

The phrase "have gone out," indicates that they had been members of the Christian fraternity, and had used their place in the Church as a vantage point for the propagation of false teachings. In I John 2:19 we read of certain ones—perhaps these same—"they went out from us, but they were not of us; for if they had been of us they would have continued with us; but they went out, that they might be made manifest that they were not all of us." In other words, men who confessed loyalty to Jesus Christ became apostles of another gospel, the advocates of anti-Christian teaching. Even modern warfare, with all its devices for the destruction of an army, has been able to hit upon nothing more effective than to get an enemy within the camp. No men in all England are able, today, to do her injury as those men who dwell within her borders, even joining her army, wearing her uniform, but secretly communicating with and aiding her enemies. The word "spy" has long been a detested one. As a rule, a man who plays that rôle is not held in esteem by any save those whose interests he directly represents. Paul, writing a letter to the Galatians, declared that he had encountered "false brethren, brought in unawares," who came in privily to spy out the liberty he and his friends enjoyed in Christ Jesus, and bring them into bondage.

We do not desire to be harsh, nor uncharitable; but we must declare our deepest conviction, namely, that the greatest enemy of any Church of Jesus Christ is the man who remains in her, assumes to be one of her teachers, calmly wears her good name, and yet denies the deity of Him who brought her into being, and disputes the authority of the Book upon which she has rested her every contention. I regard myself as declaring a most patent truth when I say that "modernism"—so-called—is just such an enemy. By lip and pen, it has alike rejected Jesus (whom John describes) and repudiated the Bible.

It is a matter of more than passing interest, also, to trace the parallelism between the opponents of John's description and the present-day opponents of Jesus.

*They Denied His Physical Manifestations.*

The language in which John indicted them is this: "They confess not that Jesus Christ is coming in the flesh." The King James version, as you recall, has it, "is come in the flesh." If that translation were correct, it might refer to the first appearance of Jesus. If the text of the 1911 version is correct, "who confess not that Jesus is coming in the flesh," then the second coming is in the mind of the sacred writer. But in either event, that which these false teachers opposed was the physical manifestation of God in Christ Jesus. Truly they have their successors. "God manifest in the flesh" is a miracle of such transcendent import as to be utterly rejected by our advocates of evolution! They almost universally resort to the statements that Jesus, while being God's best representative, was yet born of Mary and begotten by Joseph. The Virgin birth, is doubtless one of those "New Testament concepts" which, says one of their number, "the modern world, under the domination of science, finds it impossible to understand, much less to believe." Concerning the second appearance of Jesus in personal, visible form, known

## Modernism a Real Menace?

as Messianism, we are blithely told by the same writer that "it is a survival of Judaism and its influence and implications must be removed before we can see the essential elements of the gospel." Of course the resurrection of Jesus is another physical manifestation, which, while not expressly mentioned in the text, is involved in the question; and, it is now well nigh the common custom among "new theologians" to hold that New Testament contention to ridicule. In fact, we are plainly asked the question, "If a man believes in a risen Christ without believing in the events of the first Easter Day, or in the objective character of the appearances of Jesus to Paul and the other apostles" should "he be excluded from preaching the gospel of salvation?" and answered, "assuredly not!", and are told that "he, too, can bring and must bring his conviction of the continued life of Jesus to bear upon men and women."

But this raises the logical and inevitable question, "What Jesus is he preaching, and whence does he bring either his Master or his message?" Manifestly it cannot be the Jesus of the Bible, for He was "flesh and blood" before His crucifixion, and "flesh and bones" after His resurrection, physical and visible in His ascension, and destined to be visible and personal in His glorious second appearance! What nonsense, then, to imagine that by the adoption of a name to which there was never a corresponding reality, one has created a personality and provided a message. Coningsby Dawson's poetry is the essence of inanity:

"If He lived or died, I may not know,
 For who shall disprove the words of the dead,
 Or who may approve of the wisdom they said?
 For me, He is not of the long ago,
 But speaks in the morn of my life, I know."

Who speaks, and what does he say? Is it not true, as one of their own company has confessed, that "when we take away the historical Jesus, we take away the only Jesus" and "remove the gospel," and thereby "change the very definition of Christianity itself"? "Christianity as an embodiment of the gospel is a phase of religion determined by historical facts." Any Jesus, not begotten by the Holy Ghost, born of Mary, crucified on Calvary, raised the third day, ascended to the right hand of God, and destined to descend to the earth and take His throne and reign from sea to sea, is as much the figment of a distempered imagination as are the dreams resulting from an overdose of meat; and any message based upon it has no more claims upon intelligent, thinking men than do the unintelligible, incoherent babblings of a Mary Baker Eddy. What would you think of a man who said he believed in George Washington, but not the George Washington who was born in 1732 in Westmoreland County, Virginia, who was the first President of the United States, who led in the Revolution, and whose opinions gave rise and final form to the very constitution of the country itself; he believed rather, in a Washington who never had a visible, physical existence, but whose ideas and spirit dominated the colonies in the Puritan days, and still lives. Candidly, one finds it difficult to be patient with men who name themselves "Rationalists," while dispensing with reason, and call themselves "thinkers," while giving proof that they are incapable of clearly stating premises or reaching logical conclusions. There never was a more just and justifiable indictment made against men than I. M. Haldeman brings against these self-named Moderns when he says:

"The Christ they preach never rose from the dead in the body!

"The Christ they preach has no body!

"Their Christ is a boneless and fleshless Christ!

"The Christ of the modern theologian is an immaterial ghost!"

Over the doors of some modern theological institutions might well be written, "Erected to the Ghost-Christ!"

Over the pulpits of some modern preachers might be written, "Here the Ghost-Christ is preached!"

He is a phantom of mortal mind! Their message is as baseless as their Christ is bodiless!

*These Teachers, John Denominated the Antichrist.*

His language is: "This is the deceiver and Antichrist. Look to yourselves, that we lose not those things which we have wrought, but that we receive a full reward."

A careful study of the Bible will show that the Antichrist is a person destined to head up the final but fatal rebellion against God; and yet the Sacred Scriptures equally teach that preliminary to his appearance and preparatory unto the same, is a whole school of men who shall speak against Jesus Christ, incessantly striving to bring God to the level of man, and to exalt man to the height of God.

Fundamental to this whole Satanic scheme is the discrediting of the Sacred Scriptures. The man who attempts that is brought to book in John's catalog of the Antichrist. Before one can successfully dispute the claim that "Jesus is the Son of God, that God dwelleth in him, and he in God," he must discredit the whole doctrine of inspiration; and yet, unless he do that adroitly, he may fail even in the judgment of his coveted followers. What could be more adroit than to insist that the denial of inspiration is not necessarily a denial of a divine Saviour? They tell us that Jesus is the foundation of our religion, and whatever else we lose we shall not lose Him. It is written, "Other foundation can no man lay, than that that is laid, which is Jesus Christ." But back of foundation-laying is work in the quarries. The Scriptures are the quarries of truth. Destroy them and no Christ can be chiseled out. Destroy them and no Christ remains save that moral phantom of the Modern's intellect. If a man bow before "Him" or "It" he must concede Mrs. Eddy's contention that our behavior is determined by the "illusions of mortal mind," and at once and forever part with the whole goodly company of New Testament apostles and teachers, for in the language of John McDowell Leavitt, "that company of notable names knew Jesus Christ by the same sufficient crowning proofs the chemist employs when he analyzes salt, the geologist uses when examining a rock, the astronomer engages when he observes the stars,—namely, the senses. These witnesses affirmed that they had seen and heard and touched Jesus both before and after the resurrection. To the visible, the audible, and the tangible they gave evidence with their blood before the earth and heaven, and with it, they sealed their testimony. Thus their sincerity is unimpeachable, while they witnessed not to a philosophical opinion, not to a scientific explanation, not to a religious dogma, but to the plain, perceptible fact that Jesus arose from the dead and ascended into glory."

The author of our text voices it after this manner: "That which was from the beginning, which we have heard, which we have seen with our eyes, which we have looked

## Modernism a Real Menace?

upon, and our hands have handled of the Word of Life: that which we have seen and heard, declare we unto you" (I Jno. 1:1-3). He it is that says: "Deny that and you are deceivers and of the Antichrist," and do become,

### The Propagandists of Infidelity.

"Whosoever goeth onward," as the expression in the original is, "and abideth not in the teachings of Christ, hath not God."

It is a significant fact that in the very word here employed, "proagon," and correctly translated "goeth onward" we have the term "progressive," which has been voluntarily assumed by the critics of the times.

*They profess to be the solitary progressives of the hour.*

They speak of themselves as "men who really think." In their advanced circle they claim to include "practically every Biblical teacher in the world of any scholarly significance." In youth, their mothers must have told them that if they did not think well of themselves no one else would, and then forgot to warn them against its too vociferous expression. Against the "Thus saith the Lord" of the conservatives, they have set up a sacramental phrase, namely, "scholarship is agreed." If they ever name an exception, they are careful not to name more than one, or at most two, who are not trailing with this self-elected tribunal.

In spite of the fact that some of us are privileged to minister to many men who represent the most complete scholastic training and who, in circles of their respective sciences are widely known and justly honored, and whose loyalty to the authority of the Scriptures and the very deity of Christ is as unswerving as was that of Paul, it is even denied that the church "now numbers among its members any considerable company of the scientifically trained and professional classes." We are asked "what has become of these college-bred men and women who went out from graduating classes into the wide world?" Possibly these Progressives might make a discovery if they sat down and studied the membership roll of the greater churches of this land, which are, almost without exception, under conservative leadership. If it be true "that in the church at large, not one in fifty members are college graduates," it might bring another revelation than that which our Progressives imagine. The discovery may be made that the conservative churches far exceed this proportion. The speaker knows well one church that multiplies this number many times over, and bears testimony that these college and university men and women are not only among his most capable members, but are notable in their theological conservatism. It is not "education" that is taking the generation away from the church, but it is skepticism,—masking under the name of scholarship.

It is as impossible to make science oppose Scripture as it is to compel God to contend against Himself; and, if culture oppose the church, then the child fights its own mother, yea, even the creature contends against its Creator. But "Science falsely so-called," has bespattered the pages of Scripture with interrogation points, and many a college and university student has thereby stumbled. Darwinism, a dogma without scientific data, or, in the words of the famous French scientist Fabre, "A theory exploited in big words but destitute of even little facts" has undone alike the superficial student of both Scripture and science. It is impossible to start from false premises and reach true conclusions. If, therefore, we have been able, as charged, to create a test of church membership that "compels a man, under the influence of today's scholarship, to abandon not only a life of evil thought and evil action, but also the results of his education," it may be because that education was as far wrong as either his thought or action. The outcome will not only vindicate the church, but re-enthrone the Christ.

*Exclusive Leadership on the part of Moderns is a mere assumption.*

Mrs. Eddy, however, has illustrated the fact that you may state a thing so positively, and repeat it so often as to bring the superficial to accept it. She took two of the noblest words known to human speech, "Christian" and "Science" and by combining and adopting them has brought the unthinking to imagine her an expert in both; and that, in spite of the fact that her writings reveal no knowledge whatever of either.

For fully fifteen years, or longer, our self-styled "Moderns" have been asserting their leadership alike in "science" and "Scripture." Some have supposed that a thing so often spoken must necessarily be so, and so Modernism has accomplished its following! Such students would have been profoundly impressed by the Pharisee's prayer, and from the hour of its utterance, would have been his devoted followers. The claim of "assured results" has made its easy dupes in both the mining-enterprise and the hyper-critical profession. Almost without exception the devotees of that modern skepticism which discredits the deity of Jesus Christ and questions the authority of the Bible, are either still in their tender youth or else had their thinking fatally twisted before they were far out of their teens. Not once in a hundred instances do mature men turn from conservatism to liberalism, and in that instance, the rule is that while the man was mature in years, his early education was both poor and partial, and at forty he had only the intellectual equipment of a lad at twenty. Who knows a single man in whom ripened years and scholarship have combined to produce a skeptic? But there are scores of men, many of them world-famed, in whom additional study and experience have wrought an utter revolt from the doubts of youth.

But the greater seriousness of all this, John does not disregard.

*He charges those who reject the Son with having lost the Father also.*

Unitarianism, masking under the term

"evangelical," proposing to retain God, even though Christ be rejected, has no God, unless John be disputed. "He that hath not the Son hath not the Father." "Whosoever goeth onward and abideth not in the teaching of Christ, hath not God."

The New York Presbytery, in ordaining men who dispute the virgin birth, and thereby deny the inspiration of plain Scripture statement, if it continue to wear the name of "Christian" will do nothing better than cloak an infidel form with a profession of faith. The life of Presbyterianism, as a positive Christian force, will depend in no small measure upon its eventual regard for the Cincinnati Presbytery's request that such Unitarians be disfellowshiped. The history of the past has provided abundant proof of the utter powerlessness of the Unitarian propaganda. It has created no ministry worthy of mention, it has started no missions that have proven virile, it has established no colleges that play conspicuous part in the educational process. It has affected so few converts from sin to holiness that one sometimes wonders how it keeps courage enough to build an occasional church. Its people are almost universally disciples of Charles Darwin, and with equal unamity they emasculate the writings of Moses, repudiate all the prophecies of Daniel, and laugh to scorn the Apocalypse of John, while Jesus is to them Mary's bastard son. Is it any wonder that John dares to say "Whosoever goeth onward and abideth not in the teachings of Christ, hath not God"?

But now what is to be the attitude of true Christian men and women toward all of this? Let John speak again, "If anyone come unto you and bring not this teaching, receive him not into your house, nor bid him Godspeed, for he that biddeth him Godspeed is partaker of his evil deeds."

### The Participants in the Antichrist.

According to John, *Christian fraternity is not for Christ's opponents.* One of our best commentators tells us that the phrase "If anyone come unto you and bring not this teaching, receive him not," looks not to a social reception, but, rather, to a reception into the house of God unto Christian fellowship. The true Christian will not be unfriendly toward an infidel, nor refuse social fellowship with a skeptic. On the contrary, he will show neighborliness for every man visiting his door, and kindness to any one coming to, or going from the same. But that does not mean his reception into the fellowship of God's family, nor a benediction upon infidelity in God's name. I have no creed to which my neighbors must subscribe, no doctrinal standards to which my acquaintances must come. The Unitarian may be my closest personal friend, and the Universalist my fishing companion, and it is alike my privilege and pleasure to return the bland smile of Mrs. Eddy's disciple. But the fellowship of faith is altogether another thing, and cannot be accorded to any who "bring not the teaching of Christ"—"God manifest in the flesh." The moment you create a church that exceeds fellowship in Christ, you introduce into it the seeds of self-destruction. The weakness of present-day Protestantism is at exactly that point. We are wondering why we are not making greater progress. We are worrying over subjects of secondary concern. We are searching every nook and corner of church life to discover the elements of weakness in our work. We are saying that by "a further federation of forces" we will "engender power." The exact opposite is true! We are over-federated now. Our affiliations are our fundamental weaknesses. Better a Gideon's three hundred that believe God and lap the Water of Life from the fountains of His Word than the thousands that now leisurely drink from the tasteless springs of skepticism that gush from multiplied schools as water does from the mole holes of the Southland in a wet season.

But John has a further word,

*He Makes Our Commendation of Skeptics a Self-Condemnation.*

"He that biddeth him Godspeed is partaker of his evil deeds." Frankly do some of us confess "to making it a part of our life work to mark the man 'who brings not the teaching of Jesus—God manifest in the flesh—and to refuse to recommend him to any church seeking our advice. How can we do otherwise and keep conscience at all? Would we advise any wife to take into her house, as a boarder, a man who would alienate her affections from her husband, and by criticisms finally dethrone him from the headship of the family? Can we advise any church to receive as a pastor a man who denies the deity of Jesus, and removes from the headship of the Church her own and only rightful Lord? Believing as we do that He is the very God, the one and only basis of hope for time and eternity, the one and only sufficient moral ideal, and inspiring personality, the one and only Saviour from sin; in fact, the one and only way for the world's redemption, how can we recommend the man who proposes to tear the crown of deity from His brow, dispute His authority over the conscience and His Lordship over life?

John McDowell Leavitt said truly, "Take Jesus from the world and you turn it into gloom. Let Him reign and humanity realizes its dream of light and love. In His system and character are all the marks of a divine Messiah. But Jesus false, how black the picture and how inconceivable the consequences. No middle place for this Christ, so perfect in character and so matchless in career. If not from the Holy Ghost in the Virgin, His conception a lie! If angels did not sing at His birth, and after temptation and amid agony, and watch at His tomb, narratives of their appearances, falsehoods! If no divine voice at His baptism, His ministry of holiness opening with imposture! If no suffering mortals relieved by His touch and words, His miracles of love fabrications! If no power over Ha-

## Modernism a Real Menace?

des, His promise to the thief on the cross a deception! If no resurrection and ascension, fraud carried over life into death itself!" If no return in power, then no millennium for this world is possible, and the future will grow increasingly bloody and eventuate in the darkest of nights. He who mars the Jesus of the Bible, unmakes mankind. He who blots the sentence of sacred Scripture, flings a blackness over future history.

Commend him as a teacher? Ask a church to appoint him to its leadership? Write letters, dexterously dodging the facts involved, in aiding him to cover up his unfaith long enough to be comfortably seated and begin to uncover his skepticism, and thereby break the hearts of his aged parishioners, and destroy the faith of his youthful ones? Never! For this would be to be a partaker of his evil deeds. The compromise of truth is a crime against Christ!

The crisis is on! The injunction of Joshua lives again, "Choose you this day!"

"He that hath felt the spirit of the highest
    Cannot confound or doubt Him, or deny;
Yea, with one breath, O world, though thou deniest,
    Stand thou on that side, for on this am I."

## CHAPTER III.

## IS MODERNISM UNDERMINING THE EVANGELICAL MINISTRY?

"Thus saith the Lord of hosts, Hearken not unto the words of the prophets that prophesy unto you: they make you vain; they speak a vision of their own heart, and not out of the mouth of the Lord. They say still unto them that despise me, The Lord hath said, Ye shall have peace; and they say unto every one that walketh after the imagination of his own heart, No evil shall come upon you. . . . I have not sent these prophets, yet they ran; I have not spoken to them, yet they prophesied. . . . Behold, I am against them that prophesy false dreams, saith the Lord, and do tell them, and cause my people to err by their lies, and by their lightness; yet I sent them not, nor commanded them; therefore they shall not profit their people at all, saith the Lord" (Jeremiah 23:16, 17, 21, 32).

"Modernism" is a phrase so often employed that men imagine something is new under the sun; and many are brought to believe that the pulpits are now occupied by a company of preachers without worthy predecessors. The cry "Eureka" does not always involve a discovery. The opinion is all too prevalent that the preacher has just now been educated for the first time; and consequently become a capable man: a conclusion reached without due reference to historical facts. The founders of America believed an educated ministry fundamental. You go to the north gate of Harvard and you will read this inscription:

"After God had carried us safe to New England, and we had builded our houses, provided necessities for our livelihood, reared convenient places for God's worship, settled the civil government; one of the next things we longed for and labored for was to advance learning that we might not leave an illiterate ministry to our posterity when our present ministry shall lie in the dust."

New England Universities are almost as old as New England itself. They were founded not so much in the interest of advanced science as in the interest of progressive sanctity; not so much for the education of men in commerce and letters as for the preparation of men for the ministry. The term "Modernism" when employed to describe the educational movement of the moment, looks more to the lifting of the other professions to the ministerial level than it does to bringing preaching up to the level of other professions. And yet, that that term has profoundly influenced the ministry no man questions.

In view of this fact, I want to call your attention to the attitude of Modernism, the theology of Modernism, and the travesty of Modernism.

### The Attitude of Modernism.

The ministers who boast themselves "Moderns" may not easily consent to our characterization: and yet, if we demonstrate its justice by copious quotations from their pens, they cannot successfully discount it.

Permit three remarks to express our understanding of this attitude.

*It is an attitude of self-aggrandizement.*

The book-stores and libraries literally teem with output from the pens of Moderns; and, in the language of Edward Leighton Pell, this impression is bourne in upon the reader of these production, viz., that the authors "are victimized by the illusion that the sun never rose until the present generation of scholars came upon the stage." For instance, take the phrase already referred to, "The rise of Higher Criticism and its adoption by practically every Biblical teacher of scholarly significance in the world, is one of the most striking char-

## Is Modernism Undermining? 57

acteristics of today's religious life!" There are scores of men that can think clearly, read Greek and Hebrew easily; some of them can even dicipher hieroglyphics, and many of them give themselves to research of the most extensive sort, and have made for themselves places of international reputation; and yet, having repudiated Higher Criticism they cannot be regarded by these Moderns as teachers of "any scholarly significance." Dr. A. T. Robertson can produce a Greek Grammar and Lexicon that gives promise of putting Thayer out of commission, and yet if he speak not the shibboleth of the destructive critic, he is ruled out of the realm of scholarship. Prof. Orr could call the attention of the religious world to his masterly work, but, not being among the critics, the Modern makes no mention of him. Dr. Frederick Wright of Oberlin, outshines Oberlin's President in scholarship, but being a believer, he does not count. Prof. Ira Price of Chicago University is authority in the realm of Archæology, but being a conservative he is discounted by his own Seminary associate! We are told, with somewhat more of commiseration than sympathy, that "since Dr. Green's death conservativism is without a worthy scholar." A ruse like this always works with mental weaklings. The cowardly are always afraid their true feelings will be found out; hence their loud profession of bravery. And the mentally incapable are equally sure to covet the reputation of competents, and many a student who can never make his grades will be driven to name himself "A Modern," and to flaunt his new found infidelity in order to distract attention from his true attainments, while many another student submits to the innoculation of infidelity rather than be disfellowshiped by the gentlemen who proudly point to that scar of the soul.

*It is also an attitude of assumption.*

It assumes to be scientific. And then to make that assumption good, it presents another, namely, that "Evolution is scientific." Dr. King, of Oberlin, says "The idea of evolution became to the world a scientific reality with the publication of Darwin's 'Evolution of the Species' in 1859." A phrase like that destroys the definition of "Science" itself, for "Science is knowledge gained and verified," and confessedly Darwinism is without verification. Dr. King tells us that "there may be a deification of truth which is only the dei-

## Is Modernism Undermining? 59

fication of an intellectual formula" and observing men cannot ignore the fact that there may be "a deification" of utter falsehood, if only some noted individual name it "Truth." The land is full of little men, and crowded with boys and girls who will run as quickly at the call of some notable name and swallow as greedily anything that he may present to them, as the barn-yard hens come at the cluck of the plumaged cock. It has always been so! In young Judson's day the students of the hour greedily swallowed Deism, when the only thing in its favor was the fact that it had been exploited by some notable professors and accepted by men supposed to be scientific, and to this hour the land has not fully recovered from the effects of that unscientific infidelity. There are no more bitter fruits than those that grow on the twigs of false assumptions! Witness the sinking of the Titanic and remind yourself of the awful death-struggle in freezing waters, of a great crowd of hundreds who, under the inspiring boast of its builders, assumed that their bark was unsinkable!

Again, *the attitude of Modernism is intolerant.* We have already proven that, according to one of its notable advocates, there are now no living scholars outside its special assembly. The same writer contends that there are no schools worthy of serious consideration except they speak the shibboleth of the Modern. In treating of such institutions as the Bible Institutes at New York, Chicago, Minneapolis, and Los Angeles, he questions whether what they teach is worthy to be termed "theology" at all, and bases this criticism solely upon the circumstance that they "are opposed to modern critical thought" and are not enamored of "Hastings' Dictionary" so-called, and are even "hostile to evolution and all its implications," and are such mental mossbacks as to entertain the "Messianic hope of the primitive church." But in quieter moments this same writer passes sufficient sentence upon his own company. With little show of penitence, but with perfect pertinence, he says, "Liberalism has its dogmatism as real as that of traditionalism and often more arrogant. Its weapons are scorn and contempt. The sin that so easily besets it is impatience of criticism and opposition. It is hard for any of us to take our place by the side of the Publican and not find ourselves edging over toward where the Pharisee stands, shouting his egotistical prayer." That may be the reason for what the Advance had to say concerning the utterance of a Congregational preacher—A Modern—before the National Congregational Council, held at Cleveland a few years since. The Editor affirmed "A more bold and bald declaration of infidelity was perhaps never before heard in the presence of a religious body in this country. He denied that the Bible is the inspired Word of God and said there could be no atonement and there was no need of one. . . . He could show more scorn in a minute for the faith that has transformed and transfigured the lives of millions of men than the most sarcastic politician can show for the opposite party in a political campaign." But it should be remembered that scorn and science are not synonyms; and the Pharisee's profession of personal superiority is no positive proof of its certain possession.

This attitude of Modernism has had its effect in the realm of religion, and it has produced what we might properly name

### The Theology of Modernism.

*That theology is more philosophical than Biblical.*

In fact, the phrase to which Moderns have

committed themselves is this, "The real issues are now seen to be theological and not Biblical," an indication as clear as language can make it that Moderns propose to rest their opinions of God no longer in the sentences of sacred Scripture, but rather, in the speculations of twentieth century philosophers. Prof. Peabody, of Harvard, asserts that "theology is now the least thing required of the man who is equipping himself for the ministry;" . . . "The language of the times seems to be a call away from theology."

Some of us, listening to the talks of the later theological graduates, have long suspected this. These talks have not impressed us as having even the taint of theology about them; and the man who has a philosophical vs. a theological foundation, is commonly a man who veers with every wind of doctrine and is tossed by every wave of skepticism. Reginald Campbell never took a course in theology; his books are in no sense theological treatises; and his uncertain philosophies adequately account for his shifts from Methodism to Congregationalism, and from Congregationalism to Episcopalianism, and now gives promise of landing a philosophical Unitarian in the lap of Rome. I know three Baptist men in Amer-

## Is Modernism Undermining? 63

ica, occupying positions of importance everyone, who entered the ministry without a theological training, and during the first few years of their ministerial life, being left to themselves and the Bible, became flaming Evangels and made for themselves, in each instance, a national reputation. But that reputation became their peril and put them into touch and even fellowship with that professional crowd who always seek the fraternity of the famed; and, in this more critical and skeptical atmosphere their hold on the Bible is breaking, their confidence in the Christ of God is crumbling, their former views of "the kingdom" are repudiated,—all in consequence of the one fact that, having no theological foundation, they have been easily subject to the twisting hurricanes of modern philosophy.

*That theology boasts itself scientific rather than Scriptural.*

On his own confession, the Modern insists that his "method of religious thinking is becoming scientific rather than literally Biblical." And, he imagines by the very use of the word "scientific" that he has settled every question as to the correctness of the method. He would be at once foolish and inconsistent who denies honors to Science; on the other hand, he is a credulous individual indeed who imagines that by calling his course "scientific" he has thereby settled its correctness. Dr. Pell tells us that "the first time Paul and Barnabas did some wonderful things, the people jumped to the conclusion that they were both gods, and went into wild acclaim over them." Some men have treated the accomplishments of science after the same manner. Because it has wrought some wonderful things they have flung themselves at its feet and will have it that there is no God beside it. Our fathers hailed science with delight, but held her to be the handmaiden of religion. Many of their sons have sought, rather, to make her religion's substitute. The effect is little less ludicrous than the following regarding Malcolm James McLeod. When he had a wedding in high society he marched to the opening strains of Lohengren and took his place before the chancel, his hands clasped behind his back, a manual between them. When the music ceased and all was quiet, he opened the little book to discover the title "Todhunter's Conic Sections." But why object? Is not "Todhunter's Conic Sections" a treatise on science; and is not science now in the ascendancy; and should not preachers deal with scientific subjects? Certainly! But when you come to perform a marriage ceremony, if you have been unable to commit the service to memory, the thing you need to have in hand is a minister's manual. And some of us believe that the minister's great manual is not a treatise on science, but rather the Holy Scriptures; and if that excludes us from the company of Moderns we prefer to part from skeptical men rather than the sacred Book.

*Their theology produces preachers, but not prophets.*

Modernism, having subsidized the theological seminary, is now engaged in making the ministry of the hour, and according to the Harvard Theological Review, these ministers "administer congregations, organize ecclesiastical industries, become philanthrophists and pastors, but not theologians." It might have remarked also "and not prophets of God!" The reason is not far to seek! Modernism makes little of the Bible. In the language of Arthur S. Hoyt "All the real prophets of Christianity have been masters of the Bible." Modernism makes less of Christian experience. No prophet can ever exist who cannot at least say, with the healed blind man, "One thing I know." The methods of Modernism being destitute of the Holy Spirit have been as incompetent as their teaching has been unblibical! Frozen formalities and unoccupied pews are the inevitable output.

In that delightfully readable volume, McLeod's "Letters to Edward," he tells of a brilliant young college woman, Miss Johnson and her young friend Graham, with whom he fell in on one occasion, and gives a rather voluminous report of Miss Johnson's views of preachers in general. Among other things she says, "I think the great thing preachers ought to aim at today is to be interesting. First of all, to be spiritual and then to be interesting. The little codger who spent the day fishing without getting a bite, gave a sufficient explanation when he said, 'We did not seem to catch their attention.'" "Doctor," she continued, "dullness in the pulpit is an unpardonable sin; and yet, shall I confess it, nine sermons out of every ten are to me dull." And she goes on to speak of a professor "in one of the leading seminaries, who has a chair in Homiletics, which means, I believe," she adds, "how to preach!" "Is not that so, Doctor?" "And yet, that same man who started in the

## Is Modernism Undermining? 67

ministry with a large congregation, and in two years preached the building empty, is now teaching the young theologues how to reach the masses!"

This speech of Miss Johnson's reminds every one of us of seminary professors we know, and we marvel not that no prophets of God come from their feet. The theological students have received from them neither message nor inspiration. In fact, by turning the attention of young men from Biblical theology to Darwinian philosophy, they have taken away the source of both information and inspiration. That fact makes its manifestation in the ministry of today. The Ladies' Home Journal, for May 1916, contains on page nineteen, an analysis of 800 sermons; thirty-eight of them were Biblical-expository or textual; thirteen of them evangelistic, and the remainder had had to do with such subjects as Literature, Plays, Science, History, Efficiency, etc. Self-culture capped the climax with the number 213.

Without a message, certainly inspired, and without an inspiration consequent upon an indwelling Spirit, the prophet perishes! The most pitiful fate that ever befell a preacher is described by Dr. Pell under the name "Rev.

Hail Fellow Well-Met, widely known to the readers of the society column, as Mr. Knickerbocker's constant attendant at golf, a charming essayist at the Woman's Club, and the best local authority on the drama" as well as "a popular baseball fan," a man "who can slap more good fellows on the back and take more soft drinks at the soda fountain than any three clergymen in the city."

Doubtless Dr. Pell has occasion for this statement "We do not need jolly good fellows in the ministry. We need prophets who stand apart from the jolly crowd; men set apart unto God; men who stay in the presence of God until their faces are white with the light of God, and who hasten with His message to their fellowmen while the light is still on and the fire is still burning high in their hearts." If the theological seminary is failing to produce such men, the hour has struck to strengthen that new-born institution—the modern Bible School—the curriculum, atmosphere, and whole intent of which is set to the one purpose of producing prophets of God rather than ethical essayists or china-painting preachers.

### The Travesty of Modernism.

But after all, what is the fundamental error in Modernism? Great men, and even great movements, have succeeded in spite of the self-aggrandizement that often envelopes them; in spite of certain false assumptions, and in spite of intolerant attitudes. There must be in "Modernism" some more marked weaknesses than any of these, or even all of them combined. What are those weaknesses? Let us conclude with the fundamentals.

*Modernism puts man's word in place of God's Word.*

A man who took the finishing touches of his theological training in the University of C—— once brought to me one of his printed sermons on "Inspiration" and asked me to read it carefully and give him my judgment of the same. When he came for an opinion I had finished the task and was compelled to tell him "There is not a quotation of Scripture in it; like Darwin's Origin of Species it is a theory." How much of such preaching we have under the shadow of this boastful movement known as "Modernism!" Some writer quotes Bædeker as saying of a certain town in Italy, "You will find fresh eggs here, and butter and milk and excellent fruit, provided you carry these delicacies along with you!" If you are to attend upon the preaching of a Modern, that seems to be the only way to feed upon the gospel while there! Carry it with you, or you will go hungry!

Ancient as our text is, it never had a more direct application than now, nor pointed to a more patent truth. "They speak the vision of their own heart, and not out of the mouth of the Lord. They use their own tongues, and say, he saith. They dream dreams and tell them, and God's people do err by their lies, and by their lightness."

*They put man's work in place of God's work.*

Truly did Bishop Cheney, answering the question "Why candidates for the ministry were diminishing?" lay the blame upon the theological seminary that changed the evangelical ardor of the young student into indifference, and sent him out with the admonition that the business of the twentieth century minister was to lead in sociological reform rather than convince of sin and the need of salvation; provide a better environment to the poor rather than preach to them regeneration, substituting hygiene for heaven, food for forgiveness, country air in place of confessions of faith, and establish what Dr. I. M. Haldeman

## Is Modernism Undermining?

defines as an "Institutional Church," wherein you can "secure anything desired from a sermon to a sandwich, and from theology to the theatre . . . The Church that is taken up with everything under heaven except the message direct from God and by God," where "every man hath a psalm and every man a doctrine," where "the modern machinery has ground out the moving Spirit, and the organization itself has dispensed with God—Churches of the Laodicean type, churches perfectly organized and up-to-date, but with the Christ outside." That is the thing that makes Modernism a moral and spiritual menace, and constitutes a rallying cry to every friend of the Bible and Christianity to come at once to their defense.

*Modernism has taken away the minister's Christ.*

It has denied the Virgin birth! It has disputed His miraculous works! It has resented His claims of resurrection, and scorned His reputed ascension to the right hand of God, and it despises His promised re-appearance in power and glory.

To be sure some of its advocates deplore these positions, denominate them "extreme," yet they have become so common as to make up an essential element in its nature and character. Its devotees increasingly "deny the Christ who bought them." Imagine the consequences to the churches that receive such a ministry and the effect upon the lives of young men and women who, in the student days, are attracted and taken by its tinsel show of science and its false promises of mental and social premiums.

I never think of that great student body that throngs the halls of college and university, female and theological seminary, but to remember what soul-dangers they are sure to encounter, and to be reminded afresh of Beckford's "Vathek." You recall it! "The games of the day went forward with all alacrity, and at length concluded just as the twilight began to overcast the mountain; and Vathek, easily the leader of the hour, was still standing on the edge of the chasm, and suddenly called out with all his might, 'Let my fifty favorites approach me separately; and let them come in the order of their class. To the first I will give my diamond bracelet; to the second, my collar of emeralds; to the third, my aigret of rubies; to the fourth, my girdle of topazes, and to the rest of them portions of my dress.'

## Is Modernism Undermining? 73

The direction was received with acclaim, and all extolled the liberality of a Prince who would thus strip himself for the amusement of his subjects and the enjoyment of the rising generation. The Caliph in the meantime undressed himself by degrees, and raising his arm as high as he was able, made the diamonds glitter in the air. But whiles he delivered it with one hand to the child who sprang forward to receive it, with the other he pushed the poor innocent into the chasm where the Giaour, with a sullen muttering, incessantly repeated, 'More! More!'" Then Beckforth remarks, "This dreadful device was executed with such dexterity that the boy who was approaching him remained unconscious of the fate of his forerunner; and as to the spectators, the shadows of evening precluded them from perceiving any object distinctly. Vathek having in this manner thrown in the last of the fifty, and expecting that the Giaour on receiving them would present the key, already fancied himself as great as Soloman, and consequently above being amenable for what he had done; when, to his utter amazement, the chasm closes and the hole was as smooth as the rest of the ground."

It is a frightful thing to say, but I do not

believe there ever was a more perfect parable presented in literature, if it be but applied to that professor who holds before the eyes of ambitious young men and women the diamond glitter of so-called scientific knowledge, the emerald light of promised efficiency, the ruby red of gratified tastes, the tango girdle of acquired gold, until the very Adversary that waits to destroy them, is both denied and disdained. Nor do I think there ever was a more perfect parable of the engulfing plain of skepticism, now existing in such schools as permit the Bible and spiritual experiences to be laughed at, and even the saving power of Christ to be denied! Let me call every young man and young woman who has honored me with audience to turn from such a Caliph's field to the cross of Christ, and tell you what that cross, even though it be weakly interpreted and poorly understood, may do for every one who looks upon it. A young woman lay in our city jail, incarcerated for nameless crimes. Girls from the church went to her cell and talked to her of Christ and His cross. Once they were out of her sight she raised a clinched fist and stamped her foot and said, "The cross be damned!" Leaning forward she looked between the iron bars through the open win-

## Is Modernism Undermining? 75

dow; and lo, in the very heavens, as it seemed, there glowed the great cross outlined by electric bulbs on the top of the Wesley Methodist Church. At the sight of it she screamed "The cross!—The cross!" and sank, unconscious, to the floor. When she was revived, they explained to her that she had seen no vision from heaven, but merely an advertising sign. To this she responded with intelligence, "I care not who put the sign there; God has spoken to me through it, and never again will I willingly sin against the Christ of the cross." From that moment she has walked in the ways of righteousness and joined in intelligent service to the Son of God. Any education that takes the cross from the sin-cursed world is nothing short of a soul-tragedy! Such schools as accomplish that crime in the name of culture, were better wiped, at once, out of existence!

## CHAPTER IV.

# HAS THE STATE UNIVERSITY BECOME A HOT-BED OF HETERODOXY?

"Render, therefore, unto Cæsar the things which are Cæsar's; and unto God, the things that are God's" (Matthew 22:21).

Has the State University become a hot-bed of heterodoxy? Before attempting to answer that question in any measure, let me make plain some secondary matters.

First of all, I have no personal grievance against the State University, nor any phillipics against an institution which is justly esteemed, and is splendidly efficient. I am a stockholder in the State University of Minnesota. It is not the institution of the Board of Regents; it is not the institution of the faculty, it is not owned by the student body; it belongs to the citizenship at large, and it ill becomes any man to speak against his own.

There are a great many of us who object to the combination of Church and State; but that does not mean that we are all for the

Church and all against the State; it merely means that each has its place in human society, its separate part to perform; and, while there are many necessary instances of over-lapping, there are no necessary points of antagonism. When such exist, either the Church or the State, or both, are wrong, and it then becomes necessary for the individual to discriminate and choose.

There is a story told of Tolstoi that one day in Moscow he saw, near one of their famous gates, a persistent beggar, asking alms, and loudly exclaiming, "A little penny, brother, in the name of Christ." Just as this appeal smote Tolstoi's ears a police officer,—young, martial, and commanding, approached. Thereupon the beggar fled! Tolstoi looked into the officer's face and said, "Brother, can you read?" "Yes," said the officer politely. "Have you read the Bible?" "Portions of it" replied the officer. "And do you remember Christ's orders to feed the hungry?" "Yes," said the officer.

"And now, may I ask, Can you read?" "Yes," replied Tolstoi. "Have you read the police regulations?" "Yes" was Tolstoi's answer. "And do you remember that begging in the main streets is forbidden?"

When the course of this world and the

Word of God are in conflict, the individual is compelled to choose; and unless the public is altogether mistaken, certain State University professors are creating more and more a conflict between the evangelical church and the modern State; and are, thereby, producing effects, which some of us regard as deleterious to both Church and State; hence the necessity of this discourse.

But let me add another word before entering fully upon some definite themes and propositions. After twenty years of observation upon the State University I am fully persuaded that more than one half of its professors have no controversy with either the Christian Church or its Sacred literature,—the Bible. It is a custom, however, centuries old, for unbelievers to be blabby! Considerable fuss comes as easily from the lips of infidelity as smoke pours from a chimney.

I pass over, therefore, that great body of grand men who make up the real strength of the State University, and purposely elect to speak of that small but more vocal company who use the University professorship to exploit infidelity; and I lodge against them three indictments! They are inconsistent; they are incompetent; and they are irreverent!

## Inconsistent.

*They exercise, as their right, that which they refuse to others.*

They are set to teach Biology, Botany, Sociology, or History; they essay to speak on the authority of the Scripture, the Deity of Christ, heaven and hell, and whatever religious subjects they like. The moment, however, a minister invades their realm they resent it, and remind the pupils "He is only an ignoramus in realms of Science." Evidently it does not occur to them that the minister, if he be educated at all, has spent at least four years in the study of these scientific subjects; and in case University instruction has been worth anything, he has at least a basis of opinion upon scientific subjects. But when did instructors in Science study Scripture at all; and where? What fitness have they to pass sentence on Scripture subjects? I was present recently in a University, and was waiting my time to address the faculty and students at the chapel hour when a young professor in cap and gown, set on that special morning to the task of leading the devotional exercises, got up from his chair, walked with great importance to the desk, announced a song, and backing up sat down again quite demurely. The hymn once sung, he walked forward with equal importance and said, "Let us pray," and started in to lead the company in what is known as "The Lord's Prayer." At the middle of it his memory slipped a cog, and there was an embarrassing hesitation. He finally remembered the next word and started again, to balk twice before he could finish it; and yet, I have little doubt that in his class room he could speak "ex cathedra" upon sacred subjects, owing to his prestige as a professor and his consequent privilege of delivering his own judgment in the presence of boys and girls who did not feel at liberty to reply; and at a somewhat safe removal from the minister who is an expert in that branch of learning.

The minister, however, is always a welcome voice with skeptical professors, provided he speaks their shibboleth. When Rev. John C. Kimball writes a book entitled "The Romance of Evolution" and makes "a god of science greater than any of the gods old Olympic knights ever imagined," and proves himself a devotee of Darwin rather than a defender of the Divine Son of God, he is received with as much warmth as though he wore a cap and gown. That same circle of skeptical professors literally spew out the conservative preacher, but a crowded sanctuary is a gentle reminder that they do not thereby silence him, or even keep University men from sitting at his feet.

No more consistent is the custom, common with this somewhat critical company, of resenting "all assumptions" about the Bible, or about Jesus of Nazareth, while daring to rest their entire philosophy of life upon "an assumed foundation." Darwinism is a theory, not a demonstration; a speculation, not a science; and yet it is confessedly the foundation of so-called modern history, philosophy and science, and having begun in assumption, skeptical teachers are not troubled when they continue on the same basis.

In Minnesota State University Menzies' "History of Religion" is a text book, and Menzies writes after this manner: "We shall not pretend to set out on this enterprise without any assumptions. The first and principal assumption we make is that in religion, as in other departments of human life, there has been a development from the beginning even until now, and that the growth of religion has gone on according to the ordinary laws of human progress." From that point to the end of his book it speaks far more often in the language of assumption than in terms of science. It assumes, for instance, that religion is the output of civilization, when history attests that the opposite is true. The Fiji Islanders had no civilization until the Christian religion was preached among them!

Menzies comes eventually to the conclusion that Christ is the greatest exponent of religion yet appearing upon the face of the earth, without at all consenting to His deity—the only sane explanation of His infinite influence. In other words, the upshot of the whole matter is exactly what Reginald Campbell (once notorious, now seldom mentioned) voiced in his "New Theology," namely that according to the Bible "God made man in his own image;" according to Modernism, man has returned the compliment, "and made God in his image." The God of Menzies is as absolutely an evolution from some mental monad that moved in the brain pool of an anthropoid ape as man himself is an evolution from that first life cell, the ancestry of which is unexplained and inexplacable. When you invade the minister's realm to teach the young people who go from his parish such "assumptions," do not deny his right to resent it and say to those same young people "Such an explanation of the universe is inane; it reduces one to the absurdity of a creation without a Creator; thought without a Thinker; designs without a Designer; power without a Personality; angels and men without a God!"

But permit me to remind you of the second point of inconsistency upon the part of such professors:

*They pass judgment against the Scripture without granting it a hearing.*

The Bible is not to be read in State schools in Minnesota and other commonwealths, if you please. State law is interpreted to oppose it. But in the judgment of some men, the moment you don a cap and gown, the Book you cannot read, you can rip! Think of teaching young people who have never made any special study of the Bible that "the nation of Israel and the religion of Israel came into the world at the same time," and that "the tribes retained their separate gods and religious observances;" and "families among them had their own family cults;" but that "Moses was great enough to inspire in them all a kindred enthusiasm; and united them on one God,

Yahwek, or Jehovah." Think also of telling them that the early Psalms contained the mention of many "gods;" and that only the later ones declared exclusively for Jehovah. This is the thing for which the text book (Menzies) —"The History of Religion" stands, and the interpretation that is often put upon the Bible by men who talk about it; but was never found in the Bible by men who know the Book at first hand. I. M. Haldeman says truly, "In this way, every day, thousands of the young men and women of the land are being led to repudiate the God of the Bible and the standards of the Bible. Thousands of the very flower of our youth are being taught insidiously to set aside every law and precept which does not give full and personal liberty, and are being led to believe that they are in themselves as the throne of God and the final tribunal."

The greatest calamity that has befallen the modern state is the legislation against the reading of the Bible in State schools. That legislation has taken away from the modern student familiarity with the finest specimen of the English language. That legislation has taken away from the modern student the only volume on moral philosophy sane enough to stand the test of centuries. That legislation has taken away from the modern student familiarity with the fundamental laws of all advanced civilization—the only adequate moral codes to be discovered in human history. That legislation has taken away from the modern student the one Book which has inspired more men to great endeavors, and made more women of great character than all the remaining volumes of the millenniums of human history put together. I insist that to pass sentence against the Bible without permitting it to speak for itself is a wicked inconsistency, and is unworthy a man fit for any professor's chair.

> "A glory guilds the sacred page,
> Majestic like the sun,
> It gives a light to every age,
> It gives but borrows none.
>
> "The hand that gave it still supplies
> The gracious light and heat:
> Its truths upon the nations rise:
>     They rise, but never set."

But permit a third remark, *These same men profess non-partisanship and practice an utter partiality.* The State University is supposed to represent the entire people. The Believing minister's interest in it is fundamentally as large as that of any man in the State; and yet there is but one way, apparently, for him to secure even the nod of recognition by skeptical administrators, and that is to adopt the philosophy and theology of Modernism. That once done he is as much in demand by school circles as his more conservative brother's services are in evangelical churches. Failing in that, his voice must be silenced! The preacher who ministers to a hundred and fifty people Sunday morning, and fifteen Sunday night, is an accepted spokesman at the University chapel if he speaks the Darwinian shibboleth; but Paul Rader, himself a college man, addressing every Lord's Day more than five thousand people who crowd to hear him, has about as good a chance to be heard in a Turkish harem as to be invited to speak within the precincts of a modern State University. Grattan Guinness, the famous founder of Harley House, originator of the great Congo Mission, author of many books, preacher of world fame, was positively refused an audience by the powers that were in a State University, while the skeptical head of one of the most skeptical theological seminaries of the denomination to which Grattan Guinness belonged was brought a few hundred miles, at the

State's expense, that students might sit under the shower of his mental sparks and hear the Scriptures discredited. Not one minister of all those coming to Minnesota in the twenty years of my pastorate here, no matter how great his influence or following, has ever been asked to appear on any State University occasion to take part in the exercise thereof, provided he was known as a radical conservative.

"Taxation without representation" once affected a Revolution in America; the present generation is more peaceful than were their Puritan fathers; and some of us believe, correspondingly more puerile.

But inconsistencies on the part of men are so common that this is not a matter of such moment as that suggested by our second remark.

### Incompetent.

There are a few principles upon which thinking men are pretty generally agreed. Let me make mention of two or three of them.

First of all *Special study is essential to intelligent understanding* That principle the average professor of the University often exploits; but he is particularly reminded of it when a man from some other department of learning enters his domain. I do not blame him! If one is to say much of biology, he ought to be a fairly good student of biology. If he is to say much of botany, he ought to be a fairly good student of botany; if he is to say much of sociology, he ought to be a fairly good student of society; if he is to say much of history, he must be fairly familiar with history; and even an expert knowledge of English does not render him a Scripure authority unless he studies the Bible. Mr. Darwin devoted his life to the origin of species, and while he was about it lost all interest in music and declared that the esthetic, emotional side of his nature was atrophied in the process. I wouldn't expect Mr. Darwin, then, to be a judge of Beethoven and Handel productions! While the Bible has to do with biology, with history, and with society, more than all the other books put together, yet many a man, studying in these realms has practically ignored its content and is therefore incompetent to pass upon its character. A recent writer says, "The other day, I ventured in the presence of my son, to make some observation upon the subject of football, and was met with fine scorn. And the scorn was righteous!

I had never seen a game of football; I had never put my foot inside the gates; I did not know a quarterback from a canvasback." And all that we ask is this—should we expect those men who have little more information regarding our religion than we have upon football to be experts upon the subject of Christianity? I heard of a city girl awhile ago who went to the country to visit. They had milk on the table and she went out and saw the man milk the cow. It was the first time in her life she had witnessed such a procedure. The next day they had honey, and the sweet girl innocently said, "Oh, do you keep a bee also?" We cannot help laughing at her, but we have no right to blame her. But if she sat down to write a book upon the beehive, or even cast reflections upon honey-making, then her blame would begin. The greatest students of the Bible the world has ever seen are the greatest believers in that Book; while those who know least about it, doubt it most. The men who have given the most time to the consideration of Jesus of Nazareth have accepted Him as their divine Lord; those who study Him least, doubt His deity most; and this seems to be a sufficient illustration of the righteous principle that special study makes for the most intelligent understanding.

There is another principle equally righteous, namely this—

*Sympathetic approach invites the secrets of any science.*

The time used to be when Germany was the land of faith. For the last fifty years Germany has been equally famed as a land of "infidelity," under its new guise of "Advanced Thought"—"Higher Criticism" now named "Modernism!"

What has affected it? The modern German looks much like his fore-fathers. He is the same stockily built, square-headed individual; but the Bible does not speak to the modern German as it spoke to his illustrious sires; it does not say the same things to him it said to them. It no longer commands him as it used to command them.

What is the reason? You look into the Bible and find it has not changed a whit. Lower criticism has not changed the one thousandth part of it, and Higher Criticism has not unsettled one of the sixty-six books. Is not the difference solely the result of the attitude of scholars? The German sires approached the Bible reverently; the modern

German sons approach nothing with reverence.

To those fore-fathers the Bible revealed its sweetest secrets and resulted in the richest spiritual experiences! Martin Luther was simply a product of that spirit; but, alas for the religious havoc wrought with and by their descendants! And yet, when in the University you have your side reading suggested, I notice two-thirds of the names sound like the Teuton headlines of the morning paper; the Vons are there, and the Maxs are there, and the Vans are there, and if you take the other end of the names, the hoffs and hoffers are there; and the havoc wrought on the battlefield of faith is more to be deplored than the devastation of Belgium or the destruction of Poland, or the crucifixion of Armenia. One of the cruelest things about war is that it fattens on the flesh of beautiful boys; but infidelity, more cruel still, is no respecter of sex, but feeds by the destruction of sons and daughters alike. The man, therefore, who cannot sympathetically approach the Sacred Scriptures is by that fact unfitted to be a teacher of young men and women who dwell in a land that has received all its light from this Sacred source.

But we take an additional step—*A Spiritual experience is fundamental to Scripture study.*

The Bible itself declares the "natural man receiveth not the things of the Spirit of God" and the Bible claims to be from the Spirit. "Holy men of old spake as they were moved by the Holy Ghost." The natural man, with the natural eye, can dissect the natural body, but when he has finished he will tell you he has found no soul. It was never expected that he should find a soul; his natural eye is not adapted to that discovery. That is no proof, however, that the soul does not exist. I cannot see the will, but all scientists believe the will exists; they take it on the ground of evidence. There are also evidences of the soul, and there are evidences of the divinity of the Bible, and there are evidences of the deity of Jesus Christ. The fact that your pocket light of science does not reveal them, then, is no proof of their non-existence. Paul Rader never said a keener thing than when in my pulpit he employed his parable of the forest. "I imagine myself the owner of a great forest of several hundred acres. The finest trees in all the land grow there. They are famous; the newspapers write them up; make mention of their height, the wide spread of their

## Has the State University? 

branches, the beauty of their proportions, the character of their wood, the splendid furniture possible from the same. Herr Professor falls upon the news report and says, 'I will go and investigate' and at 10.30 at night, when I am ready to retire, he comes and tells me, 'I came to see your forest.' I say to him, 'My friend, come tomorrow when the sun is up and you can see it.' Whereupon he pulls out a pocket light, presses the button, flashes it into my face and almost blinds me, and says, 'I do not need to wait until tomorrow; I brought my light with me.' 'But that is not big enough.' 'Not big enough? It blinds you, doesn't it?' 'Tell me where your forest is and I will go and turn my light upon it.' And he starts away, and when he runs against the bark of a tree, he knows that he has arrived; and now he flashes his little light, and sees what looks like rafters over his head, and takes his little note book out and writes 'rafters,' 'many rafters.' And he turns it toward the ground and he sees a lot of dead leaves and brown burrs. He picks up a handful and rubs them together and says, 'Rubbish.' Then he puts his hand in his pocket again and pulls out his note book and writes 'Rubbish.' Then he presses his hand on the bark and picking off a piece, he rubs it into powder and says, 'Brittle, unfit for furniture.' And while he is writing it in his note book, he feels something moving about his feet, and not knowing that it is a rabbit scared by his light and scurrying away, he flashes it, and says 'Spontaneous life!' He picks up a fallen branch that has a few green tufts growing upon it, and he makes a fifth notation in his book, 'Life without roots; growing without any actual hold upon the ground or deriving any sustenance from it,' and with these observations he hastens back to the seclusion of his own study and writes an article on 'Forestry' and tells the people honestly what he saw and what observations he made as a scientist, and he tells them in all sincerity." What is the objection? Only this; he saw so little; his light was too small! What he needed was to wait until the sun came up and bathed and baptized and flooded that forest with light, and then he could have found out the truth about it.

But some men do not believe in the sun so long as they keep a pocket light, even though it be the Sun of Righteousness, or the illuminating Spirit of God! In fact, they hate Supernaturalism; they dote on the "Scientific;" they would prefer a pocket lamp (of their own invention) any minute to God's midday. Pardon me if I am not scared when the Herr Professor shoots his little paper wad of science at my theological form. Pardon me if even the awe that I used to feel for that same gentleman has passed in part. I have seen a little two by four preacher, who could not get four hundred people to hear him on any occasion, and who could not find a publisher in all the land that would take a manuscript from him and risk the expense of printing it, called to a professorship in a great University; and instantly he blossomed into authority on all scientific subjects; and I have seen that occur so often that I know what takes place behind the curtains, and am not deceived when the play is staged, and a fine scholar (?) faces the crowd and calls himself Prof. Edwin Booth, or Prof. Henry Irving, or even Prof. Wm. Shakespeare. Do not misunderstand me, I am not holding the title "Professor" to scorn! Lord Kelvin was a professor but he knew enough to make use of the Sun rather than trust his pocket lamp. Do not misunderstand me, Sir James Simpson was a professor, but he was wise enough to do his work in the bright day of God's revelation, rather than by the uncertain torch of modern philosophy. Do not misunderstand me, James Orr was a professor; but for him the Sun of righteousness had risen, and he walked with his face toward that Light, bathed in and baptized by it.

There never was an hour when young men and women so sadly needed to have professors with spiritual experiences lead them in Scripture study; teachers after the order of John, who could truthfully say, "That which we have heard, which we have seen with our eyes, which we have looked upon, and our hands have handled, of the Word of life; declare we unto you." How can the student follow his professor, and walk in the light except that professor be found walking in the same? And, is it different now from Christ's day, when if the blind led the blind they both went into the ditch together?

But I have brought a third indictment,

### Irreverence.

This is the exact charge I mean to make! If the young people in the University are trustworthy, if a mature observer like Harold Bolce knows what he sees and hears, then sarcasm and skepticism are alike employed in the students presence, and even pitted against sacred things.

*Sarcasm employed against sacred things is a proof of shallowness.*

Sarcasm and science are not convertible terms. If a professor in English, for instance, while his class reads Milton's "Paradise Lost" or Milton's "Paradise Regained" takes occasion to say, as one is reported, "I do not think I want to go to heaven; they wouldn't let me smoke there; and if they did, there would be no place to throw my ashes" he may excite laughter, but he is not fulfilling his office as instructor; in fact, he is reminding the thinking man of Bob Ingersoll. Bob met a friend and said "Take a cigar with me." "No," said the man, "I do not smoke!" "Then come across the street and let's have a little drink together." "No," replied the man, "I do not drink, either." "Then," said the Colonel, "let's go over to the stable and get some hay and chew that." "No," said the man, "I do not eat hay." "Then good-bye," said Bob, "you are not fit company for either man or beast!" Too bad that the man had not learned to eat hay, he would then be a fit companion for a jack-ass; or swallow liquid damnation, or suck at a cigarette, then he would have been at least company for some. But it may still be debatable whether he would have been good company for a true man. When a man objects to heaven because he cannot smoke there, some men would say, "Let him that is filthy be filthy still." God has prepared a place for him; all hell is a smoke room. As for me, I have been even in favor of doing away with smoke on the back end of a street car. I confess to you frankly that the heaven described in the Bible, "into which there shall in no wise enter anything that defileth," is far more attractive to me than one that might look somewhat like the so-called wash room of a pullman sleeper, packed with morning puffers.

But aside from all this, our insistence is that such remarks have no place in University instruction, and make no addition whatever to the information of the University student. They do remind one, however, of the small boy who had a smart dog, and a man, seeing his tricks, offered a fabulous price for him and led him away. Ere long he returned with the dog and demanded his money. He said, "I cannot get him to do anything for me," to which the small boy replied, "Mr., you can't learn a dog nothin', less you know more 'an the dog does." On the testimony of the students themselves, I know that they do not regard such sarcastic professors as imparting instruction.

But permit another remark on this general subject of irreverence.

*Skepticism employed in a State School is a moral and legal outrage.*

Menzies is not irreverent; but, considered from the standpoint of orthodoxy, he is skeptical. No one could read his book and imagine that he had any sympathy whatever with the Genesis account of creation; no one could read his book and imagine that Jesus Christ was begotten by the Holy Ghost. No one could read his book and imagine that he takes the least stock in the resurrection from the dead. No one could read his book and imagine that Christ will ever come again in person, with glory and power, to be Ruler of the world. These things are not so much opposed, as ignored. They are not treated with opposition, but with silent contempt. And yet when you go to the library and take down another one of the reference volumes, by Josiah Royce, from the pen of William James and other essayists, you will find him insisting that "it is absolutely essential to Christianity that one believe the report of the life of Christ as a Divine part of the original plan for the redemption and salvation of man. That one believe the report of His death, as the historical church has always maintained; yea, even that one believe the prologue to the fourth Gospel, which reviews His eternity and declares that He was with God, and was 'God,' and that in Christ, God was made flesh and dwelt among us."

It is not a necessity that a professor be himself a Christian; it is hardly to be expected, in a State School, that every instructor will subscribe to the formula of orthodoxy, but when one remembers that America is what she is, and Minnesota is what she is, and our State University exists, solely because the foundations of the State were laid in biblical teaching, every believing parent feels that skepticism is an attack upon the foundation itself, and is, therefore, a moral and legal outrage. Look back over the centuries as far as you will, and history attests that unbelief has never helped anything, and that skepticism has never resulted in righteousness or fruited in strength; while faith in God and His Word have produced the flowers of civilization. It is a serious thing then to either hold that faith to scorn or destroy it by skepticism.

Finally, *The education that ignores the soul is both a signal and sinful failure.*

One question surely is pertinent enough. Why is it that our great big institutions, with money back of them, are not able to produce their own professorships? Why does it happen now that a majority of the strong men of the University itself, and particularly those older men who have been tested, and whose value has been proven past dispute, were trained in schools where the religious life was positive, or else during the entire student days have been members of churches where there was a positive evangelical fervor? How does it happen that when we need a new President for the University itself, we do not pick up one of its brilliant outputs; but have announced to us, through the newspaper, that the man chosen was graduated some years ago from a small college famed for its Christian atmosphere, whose noble President was a consistent exponent of Christianty; and the entire faculty was framed much after the same manner.

In all probability he will be found to be a man in accord, now, with what is known as

"Modernism," but it is practically certain also that he has taken that on as a result of his more recent association with the critics, so that it in no wise effects the foundations that were laid in his earlier life. The truth is that the whole tenor of education has recently met with a sharp turn, and the present tendency is to make machines,—capable, fast running, effective machines; machines that can coin a mint of money; mental machines I grant you, that can master difficult situations; mental machines that can provoke admiration, and affect even astonishment. But the old method had only one thing as its objective, and that was to make a MAN. Our forefathers believed that the first fundamental in manhood was not morality even, but spirituality; it was not effectiveness but faith; it was not even greatness but godliness! In the language of a recent writer, whose book ought to be in the hand of every college student in the land, "For nearly a hundred years our poor little colleges, with no equipment, stood by their guns so effectively and did their work so well, that such a thing as a dearth of men was never heard of." Their output were statesmen whose fame will never drop from the annals of American history; physicians who converted sorcery into a science; lawyers whose high mentality was along Mosaic lines; preachers who elevated pulpits, in which they stood, to such eminence that we have been searching twenty-five or thirty years to find their successors. If we ever produce their equals again it will be when we turn from the false philosophies of materialism to the divine doctrines of spirituality. I tell you, in the language of the Master of masters, the Teacher of all teachers, the eternal President of all presidents, that they are "to seek first the kingdom of God and his righteousness" knowing that, as a result, all other "needful" things will be added; and knowing apart from that, no essential things can be retained.

I have no objection whatever to personal hygiene, but I know that personal holiness involves it and a thousandfold exceeds it. I have no objection whatever to commercial economy, but I know that any philosophy regarding it will fail unless Christ resides in the individual life and His language becomes the law of Society. I have no objection to teaching "social service"—the fad phrase of the last five years—and I certainly have no objection to its practices; but all thinking men ought to know that that practice will shortly fail except it be strengthened by individual salvation and personal consecration to Christ. I have no objection to the man who says "My religion is for this life," but I prefer for myself the religion of Jesus Christ, which provides for both this life and the life which is to come. I could personally enter a class in philosophy and listen to the instruction of the Professor there with pleasure, whether I agreed with it or not. His fine phraseology and his philosophical speculations might quite delight me, but when it comes to daily living I had rather have one word from the Lord Jesus Christ than a whole volume from his pen. And when it comes to dying, give me the confidence of the old sailor, who, as he neared the close of life, and friends at his bedside bent down their lips to his ear, and said, "Man, how are you now?" opened his eyes, and, as if coming out of a dream, said, "Oh, I am all right! My anchor holds!"

## CHAPTER V.

## DO OUR DENOMINATIONAL COLLEGES DENY THE EVANGELICAL FAITH?

"But there were false prophets also among the people, even as there shall be false teachers among you, who privily shall bring in damnable heresies, even denying the Lord that bought them, and bring upon themselves swift destruction. And many shall follow their pernicious ways; by reason of whom the way of truth shall be evil spoken of. And through covetousness shall they with feigned (well-turned) words make merchandise of you: whose judgment now of a long time lingereth not, and their damnation slumbereth not" (II Peter 2:1-3).

The question of this theme is not necessarily answered by the quotation in our text. The bolstering of special position by detached texts is a trick easily turned; but it may depend upon calling a contortion of Scripture an interpretation. President King, of Oberlin, never made a truer remark than when he said: "One of the greatest dangers of the educated man is to be found in his ability to defend more or less successfully any position. He finds it easy, therefore, as Fichte puts it, to 'go on subtilizing until he loses all power of recognizing truth' and readily persuades himself either that what he wants is true, or that all convictions are about equally justified. Yet indifferentism (to the text of Scripture) is neither breadth nor true tolerance. Shaler Mathews sanely remarks, "Indifference to doctrine will sooner or later make religion anæmic."

It shall be my endeavor, therefore, to array before you the facts; then rest the answer to our question with the individual judgment. It so happens that in this instance the facts are not in controversy; they exist in plain print. The instructors in our denominational colleges and theological seminaries have given themselves to magazine and book writing, thereby putting the attitude they maintain toward the whole question of evangelical faith past dispute. The saying of Jesus is especially applicable to these writings, and judgment upon these very professors is in this sentence, "For by thy words thou shalt be justified, and by thy words thou shalt be condemned" (Matt. 12:37).

It is quite essential, however, to clear and convincing reasoning that we adopt definitions; and there are at least two sets of words in this subject that ought to be clearly understood, "Denominational Schools" and "Evangelical faith." By denominational schools we

## Do Our Colleges Deny? 107

mean, of course, such academic, college and theological schools as are conducted by our evangelical denominations. The second phrase is not so simple.

### The Faith Defined.

At least three remarks, each to be followed by some considerable discussion, should be combined in order to make clear evangelical faith. They are these—Evangelical Christianity builds on an inerrant book; Evangelical Christianity believes on an infallible Christ; Evangelical Christianity emphasizes a spiritual experience.

*Evangelical Christianity builds on an inerrant Book.*

The Baptist denomination, perhaps the most ancient of all those that are spoken of as evangelical, has never, at any time, put forth a declaration of faith that did not affirm that "The Holy Bible was written by men divinely inspired, and is a perfect treasure of heavenly instruction, and therefore is, and shall remain to the end of the world, the supreme standard by which all human conduct, creeds, and opinions are to be tried."

As late as the year 1916, the General Assembly of the Presbyterian Church called the attention of the Presbyteries to its deliverance of 1910, which was that "It is an essential doctrine of the Word of God and our standards, that the Holy Spirit did so inspire, guide, and move the writers of Holy Scripture as to keep them from error."

Dr. Munhall, in speaking of "Methodism Adrift" reminds his readers that every man ordained a deacon in the Methodist Church, or to the ministry in the same, is asked the question, "Do you unequivocally believe all the canonical Scriptures of the Old and New Testaments?" and is compelled to answer, "I do believe them," and to take a solemn oath to "teach nothing but that which he shall be persuaded may be concluded and proven by the Scriptures."

In paragraph 33, of the General Rules of the Methodist Episcopal Church, the Bible is spoken of as "God's written Word, which is the only rule and the sufficient rule, both of our faith and practice." "The Confessions of Faith" adopted by other evangelical denominations of the land, put equal emphasis upon the inerrancy of the Bible. There may be individual churches, prejudiced and trained by critical pastors, who would gladly repudiate these "Confessions" and formulate for themselves a supposedly broader standing ground; but as yet they have not dared to do so, understanding full well that such action might result for them as it did for a certain Baptist Church of Grand Rapids, Mich.; namely in a withdrawal of fellowship. The sentence of Scripture expressing the standing of every evangelical church in existence today is found in Isaiah 8:20, "To the law and to the testimony; if they speak not according to this word, it is because there is no light in them."

*Evangelical Christianity believes in an infallible Christ.*

Take the same denominational standards and you will find their declarations concerning Christ equally unequivocal and strong. The Baptist finds in "the unity of the Godhead there are three persons, the Father, the Son, and the Holy Ghost, equal in their divine perfection, and executing distinct but harmonious offices in the great work of redemption."

In the minutes of the General Assembly of the Presbyterian Church of 1916, that Assembly calls the attention of the Presbyteries to the deliverances of the General Assembly of 1910—"It is an essential doctrine of the Word of God and our standards that our Lord Jesus Christ was born of the Virgin Mary. It is an essential doctrine of the Word of God and our standards that Christ offered up Himself a sacrifice to satisfy Divine justice and to reconcile us to God. It is an essential doctrine of the Word of God and of our standards concerning our Lord Jesus Christ, that, on the third day, He rose again from the dead with the same body with which He suffered, with which also He ascended into heaven and there sitteth at the right hand of His Father, making intercession. Presbyterians, therefore, are hereby not to license or ordain any candidates for the ministry whose views are not in accordance with this deliverance of 1910."

There could hardly be found in all the world a declaration of faith put forth by the Lutheran or Methodist denominations, or any other that is worthy to wear the name "evangelical" that does not declare for the deity of Christ in equally unequivocal terms. Henry Van Dyke, to whom believers are indebted for many admirable statements of truth, never expressed a more fundamental one than when he declared "The unveiling of the Father in Christ was, and continued to be, and still is, the paladium of Christianity. All who have surrendered it, for whatever reason, are dispersed and scattered; all who defend it, in whatever method, have been held fast in the unity of the faith and in the knowledge of the Son of God." In the language of John Watson, "The life-blood of Christianity is Christ!"

*Evangelical Christianity emphasizes a spiritual experience.*

It stands for the language of Jesus Himself, spoken to one of the finest specimens of manhood known to his day, even Nicodemus—"Ye must be born again" (Jno. 3:6). Principal Fairbairn, once contending for a continued revelation, affirmed, "Unless God be heard in the soul, He will not be found in the Word." Evangelical Christianity proceeds on the opposite line and says, "Unless God can be found in the soul, He will not be heard in the Word." "The natural man receiveth not the things of the Spirit, neither indeed can he know them, because they are spiritually discerned." President King is quite right: "Religion is a personal relation of man to God." At least that is true of the Christian religion; and has always been affirmed in every evangelical faith. No man can defend the deity of Jesus Christ or understand the word of the Lord, or mark spiritual growth until he has had John's experience and can speak "that which he has heard, which he has seen with his eyes, which he has looked upon, and his hands have handdled of the word of life." A liberal theologian recently affirmed of regeneration, "I never experienced any such a thing, and neither has any member of my family;" and then he strangely concluded, "Such an experience is not essential to a place in the Christian Church," as if the failure of one man to understand the Divine demand, abolishes the demand itself! Ward Beecher has often been spoken of as the Shakespeare of the modern pulpit, and Ward Beecher was a marvelous expositor of the Word, and Ward Beecher was one of the most efficient men known to the American ministry, and he affirmed that he had just such an experience, and dates all the spiritual successes of life to the same. It was in London in 1866 that he was addressing a missionary conference, and referring to the days when he was a theological student in Ohio, he said, "I know not what the tablets of eternity have written down, but I think that when I stand in Zion and before God, the brightest thing I shall look back upon will be that blessed morning in May, when it pleased God to reveal to my wandering soul that it was His nature to love a man in his sins for the sake of helping him out of them; that He did not do it out of compliment to Christ, or to a law, or a plan of salvation, but from the fulness of His own heart; that He was a being not made angry by sin, but pitying it. In short, that He felt toward me as my mother felt toward me, to whose eyes my wrong-doing brought tears, who never pressed me so close to her as when I had done wrong, and who would fain, with her yearning love, lift me out of trouble. And when I found that Jesus Christ had such a disposition, and that when His disciples did wrong, He drew them closer to Him than He did before—when pride and jealousy and rivalry and all vulgar and worldly feelings rankled in their bosoms, He opened his heart to them as a medicine to heal these infirmities. When I found it was Christ's nature to lift men out of weakness to strength, out of impurity to goodness, out of everything low and debasing to superiority, I felt that I had found God. I shall never forget the feelings with which I walked forth that May morning. The golden pavements will never feel to my feet as the grass felt to them, and the singing of the birds was cacaphonous to the sweet music of my thoughts; and there were no forms in the universe which seemed to me graceful enough to represent the being, a conception of whose character had just dawned upon my mind."

Evangelical Christianity has never intended that all men have their experiences after the same manner, nor that the phases of them be identical in any measure; but evangelical Christianity has never at any time departed from the declaration "Ye must be born again." It has believed and taught that a spiritual experience was essential to its very existence. And whenever and wherever regeneration is denied, there evangelical Christianity is dead.

Do our denominational colleges deny the evangelical faith?

## The Faith Denied.

It follows as conclusion from premise that, if evangelical Christianity has rested its entire contention in the authority and instruction of the Bible, then every man who opposes that opposes and denies the evangelical faith. Here the statement of a Divinity Professor

—(Baptist) is quoted, "Theology must wait for history; history must wait for criticism; criticism must wait for interpretation, and interpretation again for criticism." In other words, according to his declaration, Criticism is henceforth to determine alike our creed and our conduct, or our Christianity. That is a flat denial of the evangelical faith; and yet we confess with humiliation that our schools are today largely dominated by such sentiment.

*The Critics are capturing denominational colleges.*

It is probably past dispute that there are not three English speaking schools in the entire Northland, belonging to any one of the greater denominations, such as the Methodist, Baptist, Presbyterian, or Congregational, that are without an infection of that infidelity known as "Modernism!" In some of them it is small as yet, but a specked apple is not in savory estate. There are thousands of Christian parents in America who debate with the deepest anxiety the question "To what college can we send our children and be sure the Bible will not be discredited in their presence, the deity of Christ denied, and their spiritual lives reduced if not wholly destroyed?" Dr. L. W.

Munhall cites a number of instances where parents, with tear-dimmed eyes, have told him of how they have sent their children to Methodist schools for the purpose of strengthening the faith that was in them, to find them graduating at last, confirmed infidels. Without apology he mentions the Wesleyan University of Middleton, Conn., the University of Boston, the University of Syracuse, and other outstanding Methodist institutions. He reports a Bishop's daughter who declared that at the Boston University her faith was destroyed and it took her six months after returning to her home to feel that she was back on the rock Christ; and she declared that her experience was a common one with the girls of that college.

Paul Rader, one of the most outstanding of American ministers, was educated in a Methoist school, having entered the same intending to give his life to the ministry. When he quit it his faith was so attenuated that he turned from his ministerial intention and gave himself to business. But more mature thinking and a special visitation of the Holy Spirit, showed him the utter absurdity of that which had been taught him in the name of "Science" and brought him not only to the ministry

## Do Our Colleges Deny?

again, but to his present enviable and blessed position of ministerial power.

Our Baptist schools are little, if any better off. The greatest University wearing the Baptist name in America has, for years, kept upon its faculty men who are known to be the most outstanding infidels of the age. The President of the Baptist University of second importance in America said, in my presence, "Jesus Christ was no more an authority upon questions of modern Biblical criticism than Thomas Aquinas was upon the modern electric light." If one would know what is the attitude of a famed professor in Rochester let him read what he has to say upon "The attitude of the Modern Theologian toward Jesus Christ."

Or if he would marvel that changes so rapid as to make their accomplishment seem most unreasonable, let him consult the opinions of certain professors in either Crosier or Colgate, on the questions of Christ, the Bible, Satan, and Sin.

The effect of criticism on Congregational schools has been so pronounced that in many instances, that which was once evangelical, is now Unitarian in everything but name. The small college at Wheaton is lonesome in its loyalty. Princeton has been for a long time a sort of Presbyterian Gibraltar, but it is very generally imagined through the length and breadth of the land, that its President objected to the presence of Billy Sunday there not so much on the ground of Billy's antics as because of Billy's unswerving loyalty to the "faith once delivered" and the fair certainty that the world-famed evangelist would not fail on that occasion, to defend his faith. Almost without exception the biology professor in the present-day denominational college is an unequivocal devotee of Darwinism. In nine cases out of ten, his opposition to Moses is in proportion to his defense of evolution; and his boast in the name of "Science" commonly contains a sneer at Scripture. The age is Science-mad, and the man who speaks in the name of Science is likely to get a more cordial hearing than he who brings his message from the Book. In the language of another, "Modernism, Skepticism, Agonsticism, Infidelity, and worldliness are the inevitable results of the common teaching of our so-called Christian schools"—results, no one of which ever aided education in any form.

This couping of the college company has been accomplished for the most part within a quarter of a century. It is a result of the deliberate move made by the army of "Moderns!" The Germans are neither better organized nor more adequately equipped, nor more doggedly determined in their advance to battle than are the Liberals of this moment. In the language of another, "They press into every opening, they seek the possession of every college, University, and divinity school." They make their canons, construct their armored tanks, build their dreadnoughts, and furnish their submarines with what Peter calls "feigned" or "well turned words." In keeping with the customs of war, their victims are the young and the Belgium of their destructive action is the field of education.

*These critics are subsidizing our theological seminaries.*

When one reminds himself of the fact that Andover Theological Seminary was one of the greatest in America, with a creed of the most conservative type possible, and yet remembers that only a few years ago while putting their signatures to that creed, the professors who signed it, straightway departed to tear it into shreds, he is compelled to feel that dishonesty is not a misdemeanor in the eyes of the Modern. Union Theological Seminary is as plain an instance of this as ever characterized a denominational college; it is the perversion of the Presbyterian name to Unitarian uses without Presbyterian consent.

This has not been accomplished without rebellion in more than one place, but often t: rebellion has fallen short of revolution. Colgate has known the appeal of a considerable proportion of the graduating class to be excused from taking the theology they were getting a few years since; but their request was denied. When in Boston University a large number of young men, equipping themselves for the ministry, demanded the removal of a professor who had broken his own oath by attacking the creed of the church, and despising the authority of the Bible, and denying the deity of Christ, they were ignored by the trustees, and left to the dilemna of taking what was given them or departing the school life. Relief in that instance finally came through the power of the Bishop. There are many Baptist and Congregational ministers, and a much larger number of laymen, who have sometimes wished for a Bishop in their denomination.

There are scores of professors in theolog-

## Do Our Colleges Deny?

ical seminaries, located north of the Mason and Dixon line, whose theology would not be tolerated for two months in intelligent pulpits. Yet, as Dr. Haldeman says, "In this way, every day, thousands of the young men and women of the land are being led to repudiate the God of the Bible. Thousands of the very flowers of our youth are being taught insidiously to set aside every law and precept which does not give full and personal liberty, and are being led to believe that they are in themselves as the throne of God and the final tribunal." What then, will be the fate of our churches when they fall into the hands of men infected by such teaching?

Not content with their accomplishments, *the critics are now seeking the control of our churches.* By "ordaining committees" and "committees on relation of church and pastor" and a thousand other phrases that represent "well turned words," they are trying to find open doors for skeptical graduates. Every Pulpit Committee is sought out, counselled and even cajoled in the interest of some minister whose "modernism" has left him without a message. As yet, however, the churches are not greedy in their search for skeptical leaders. Their committees naturally turn to known conservative men for counsel. They are begging not to be unconsciously delivered into the hands of destructive critics. They are giving attention to the literature that is reaching their membership, and particularly their boys and girls. There has never been a time when the relationship of the denominational church to the denominational school was as strained as it is at this moment. In Canada I found that scores of churches were positively refusing to make further financial contribution to their own denominational University, on the ground that not all of its teachers were standing for the authority of the Bible and the deity of Christ. The day is at hand when the intelligent layman will think twice before he endows a college committed to the destruction of the faith, or gives his support to the theological seminary that despises the shed "blood" and seeks to substitute sociology. In the language of an advanced thinker, "The church that is to enjoy efficiency must first seek God. However much we need better organization in our churches we need more a prophetic ministry to lead men into fuller fellowship with God and a more thorough cultivation of the power to realize that vast spiritual reserve which lies just beyond conscious action. A municipal water system needs pipes, but it needs a water supply even more." And you know the application in Scripture concerning "water" that it "is the Word."

### The Infidelity Effected.

The result of this denial of the evangelical faith is infidelity. That comes in consequence of twin philosophies, the result of which is both deadly and destructive! They are these: first, The Scripture is made to appear the opponent of Science; and second, The Church is charged with having divorced culture.

*The Scripture is made to appear the opponent of Science.*

We are told "the struggle between traditional theology and science really exists." We are told, and that by a Baptist professor in a Baptist University, "The world of scholarship finds itself in perplexity as it listens to the authoritative word of the church. For in the New Testament there are concepts which the modern world, under the dominion of science finds it impossible to understand, much less to believe. To Paul and other writers of the New Testament the earth was flat with a series of heavens above and a great pit for the dead beneath; the relations of man and God were those of the relations of the subject of an Oriental monarchy. Sin was statutory; punishment was a matter of penalty, and justification was primarily a matter of acquittal at the world judgment."

It is just such teaching as that, that led Bishop Fowler to declare of his own denomination "the schools of the Methodist church belong more to the devil today than they do to our churches." If he had substituted the word "Baptist" or "Congregationalist" his remark would have been equally applicable. But, as Dr. James David Burrell has said, "The Word of God is now under fire! But the fires are no hotter than they have been from the beginning, and the inspired Book is destined to come forth seven times tried and without the smell of smoke upon it, for thus it is written, 'The earth shall be consumed with fervent heat and the heavens shall be rolled together as a scroll; but the Word of the Lord shall stand forever, for the mouth of the Lord hath spoken it'." Since God is the author of both the Bible and Nature, Scripture and Science rightly interpreted, will forever speak together. The man who pits them one against the other is a poor exponent of one or both.

*The Church also is charged with divorcing culture.*

The same Baptist Professor above quoted says, "The churches number among their members few of the professional, that is to say, of the scientifically trained, classes. They are composed very largely of men and women who, whatever may be their culture, are not college bred. It is, of course, to be expected that the great majority of our church members should come from just such classes because the proportion of college-bred men and women in a community is small. But what becomes of the thousands of young Christians whom our colleges and universities report as making up half of their entire enrollment? A recent census in one denomination numbering between twenty and thirty thousand communicants showed that, except in two or three churches, not one in fifty of its membership was a college graduate." And he asks the question, "Are we educating away from our churches? If we are, is the trouble with our educational system or the church?"

That is a very pertinent question. And there are two things that might be said. First, in those churches presided over by virile men, who believe in the authority of the Bible and in the deity of Christ, the proportion of college men in the membership is much larger than one in fifty; and second, the trouble is with our educational system rather than with the churches. The system itself is increasingly steeped in skepticism, and for the churches to accept this, or even compromise with it, is to accept death, for if they have no authoritative Scripture, no Christ who is God, the church has no occasion for its existence and preservation is hardly to be desired! If, on the other hand, the church holds God's revealed truth, it would be guilty of treason if it traded that truth for a lie, or by the spirit of toleration—so-called—brought it into infidel fraternity. The evangelical church is the mother of modern culture, and wherever there is a conflict between them it is the act of an unappreciative and rebellious daughter, and the direful results will be seen not alone in the injury of the Church, but in the triumph of that infidelity which will finally undo the pulpit in mind and morals as effectually as it is now undoing its subjects in Scriptural and spiritual experience.

*The educated are being doped with incredulity.*

As a father it would be my pleasure to give to my daughter the training of the oldest and most widely known of girl's schools; as a Christian I am unwilling to subject her to the skeptical atmosphere that now dominates in most of our Eastern female colleges. Martin Luther once remarked, "I advise no one to place his child where the Scriptures do not reign paramount." Recently the city physician decreed that all students in the school my daughter attends must be vaccinated. I confess to no small degree of revolt against having an impure virus forced into the pure blood of a girl in perfect health; but a thousand times over would I prefer my daughter's blood tainted, and her flesh scarred for a time, to having her mind tainted with infidelity and her soul scarred for eternity.

I believe in education, but not in an Antichristian one! I believe in Science, but not in an anti-scriptural one! I believe in the college, but not if it deny my Christ. I believe in the theological seminary, but not if it exalt skepticism and oppose spirituality.

When Christ is no longer worshiped, men will sink back into cannibalism; but where He is revered, there is safety and there alone. We are told that some years ago, shortly after the shadows of night had fallen, a missionary, making his way up the Congo River, was looking for a place to moor his boat for the night —a place where he would be safe—and was skirting the shore with keen eyes and careful movements, for he knew that many of the natives were cannibals, and to run upon them would be certain and cruel death. Suddenly there smote upon his ear the lusty voices of men, and listening, he heard:

> "All hail the power of Jesus' name,
> Let angels prostrate fall,
> Bring forth the royal diadem
> And crown Him Lord of all."

Instantly he turned the prow of his boat toward that part of the shore whence the sound came. He knew he could land there in safety; he knew that there he would find a blessed fellowship; he knew there were friends worthy of the name. Why? Because they were honoring Christ as the Son of God, and the

Saviour of the soul! No school is a safe landing for our lads and lasses where Christ is not equally lauded as Saviour and acknowledged as Lord!

## CHAPTER VI.

## IS THE MODERN BIBLE SCHOOL GOD'S ANTIDOTE TO SKEPTICISM?

"Behold, the days come, saith the Lord, God, that I will send a famine in the land, not a famine of bread, nor a thirst for water, but of hearing the words of the Lord: and they shall wander from sea to sea, and from the north even to the east, and they shall run to and fro to seek the word of the Lord, and shall not find it. In that day shall the fair virgins and young men faint for thirst" (Amos 8:11-13).

The Divine resources are never exhausted! God is never troubled over the question of the next step. The multitude of His opponents, and their apparent successes leave Him undisturbed. He may grieve the fate and folly of men, but He never fears the final issue. He knows that the future is with Him, and not with His Adversary. He may enjoin men to hold fast "the faith once delivered," but He does it for their sakes rather than His own. He has no alarm lest His truth fail from the earth, His revelation be blotted out and His name be forgotten. His concern, rather, is about the faith of men, lest it fail; about their knowledge of the Book, lest it be diminished; about their hold on the truth, lest it break, and they themselves be bruised by the fall. The real point of all inspired teaching, and the real purpose of all revealed prophecy, and the real intent of all Biblical preaching is the salvation and sanctification of man, not the mere retention and defense of the truth. Skepticism, therefore, does not endanger the Bible; it endangers the people! It can never unsettle the throne of God, but it always has weakened and destroyed its own disciples and apostles. The experience of Israel was the truth of yesterday; but it also is the truth of today. This text from Amos had its application to the Israel of the past; but it also has an application to the present.

It involves three significant suggestions—the Word-famine, the wander-lust, and the waiting-youth.

### The Word-Famine.

"Behold, the days come, saith the Lord God, that I will send a famine in the land, not a famine of bread, nor a thirst for water, but of hearing the words of the Lord."

The world was never in greater danger of a wide-spreading, deadly, destructive famine than it is today. If this war continues and sucks into its swirl every nation now steadily drawing toward the same, we shall have a complete fulfilment of Christ's sentence "Nation rising against nation, kingdom against kingdom, and there shall be famines." The desperate warfare being waged today is not one-half so much the expression of hatred as it is the manifestation of fear; and the thing that is feared is not the flying machine, not the armored tanks, not the submarine; these create some alarm; but the terror of the nations is "famine." Of all the enemies that man has ever faced, famine has been the most destructive; and death at its hands is as pitiless as painful; and it never works save in wholesale.

But I am to speak of another famine, namely the Word-famine. This is being brought about by such a combination of circumstances as suggests nothing short of Satanic cunning. The State schools exclude the Scriptures; the denominational schools discredit the Scriptures, the family and the individual neglect the Scriptures! That amounts to an onslaught against our Sacred Book.

*The State Schools exclude the Scriptures.*

Twenty-five years ago my wife was a student in a state University. The chapel was

## Is the Modern Bible School? 133

held every morning and was opened by Scripture reading and prayer. Now few State schools are so privileged by legal precept and still fewer so characterized by practice. In my own State, Minnesota, not a single public school teacher is permitted either to read or recite any portion of the Scriptures in the presence of his pupils. Protestant leaders have plead with politicians and Papists; but in vain! Even such excerpts as have to do with morals and ethics only, fail to receive the approval of law-makers; and the very Book that gave to American civilization its foundations becomes an increasingly unknown volume to American born or bred boys and girls.

Unfortunately, however, while Bible-loving professors are not permitted to voice the teaching of Scripture, Bible-hating ones are not denied the right of holding them to ridicule; and there are not a few state-paid instructors who exploit a skepticism calculated to create upon the child's mind the impression that the Bible is altogether an unscientific and unreliable book, and may be properly flung to the rubbish heap of superstition, credulity, myth, fable, and fetishism. The watch-word of the present hour is "Science" not Scripture; and many a teacher who is none to well versed in either makes the first contribute to a professional title, and the second to a professional titter.

*The denominational schools discredit the Scriptures.*

The late Prof. Terry published a book entitled "Moses and the Prophets" to which he attached an "Appendix" that ought to be submitted to the Mayo brothers of Minnesota and removed! It involved a diseased appendix and the case was so advanced that one wonders whether the very life of the Methodist denomination is not thereby imperilled. That appendix contains opinions from Dr. Bashford, President of Ohio Weslyan University; Dr. Gobin, of De Paw University; Dr. Plantz, President of Lawrence University; Dr. Raymond, of Wesleyan University and Dr. Warren, President of Boston University. Even Dr. Terry himself expressed surprise that, with but one exception, the views of all these men should make up a remarkable unanimity of opinion, and the man who reads them is not the less surprised, for they give pith and point to Dr. L. W. Munhall's "Breakers Ahead, or Methodism Adrift!" Removing the exception mentioned, there is not a one of them who believes in the Mosaic authorship of the Pentateuch! There is not a man of them who believes in the infallibility of the Scriptures! There is not a man of them who believes in the omniscience of Christ. Dr. Plantz, for instance, declares "It seems to me very doubtful whether Christ's knowledge extends to exact scientific and historical detail." Dr. Raymond says, "There must have been such a limitation of knowledge on Christ's part as to put Him essentially under the conditions of ordinary men."

If, in this matter, Methodism was alone, the future of the denominational school might be less discouraging; but, as a matter of fact, the appendix of Congregationalism is even more festering; while that of the Baptist denomination is in perilous estate. The President of the most outstanding Baptist University long since remarked, "No particular religious profession shall ever be held as a condition, precedent to the election of any professor to a chair in this school." Presbyterianism is our soundest sect, and yet it has repeated and acute attacks.

Many a youth, studying in our so-called Christian colleges or taking courses in our so-called theological seminaries, dwells for years in an atmosphere frigid and prayerless; for years he listens to the Bible treated, in the language of Dr. Pell "as if it were a literary patchquilt in the course of renovation," and hears Christ spoken of as if He were an "unidentified being." A. J. Gordon, for twenty-five years Boston's outstanding Baptist minister, once remarked "The heresies which have afflicted the church have almost, without exception, been invented by learned scholars, and the speculations which have blighted the faith of believers have generally been hatched and brooded in theological schools."

All of this is no argument against education! The finest religious atmosphere it has ever been my privilege to breathe characterized the Presbyterian college from which I graduated; and the most scholarly and saintly men it has been my privilege to know, instructed in the theological seminary where I took my course.

But that was twenty-five years ago! The wave of German rationalism was then beginning to beat upon our shores; now it has rolled from coast to coast, and only those men

## Is the Modern Bible School? 137

and colleges that have lived on spiritual heights, near to God, have escaped its Scripture-discrediting, doubt-deluging effects.

The companion of these adverse movements, and in some instances the result of them, exists in the fact that *the family and the individual are now neglecting the Scriptures.* We read of how the elder Spurgeon, Charles' grandfather, was so absorbed in Scripture study that when a neighbor came to visit him, he arose from his study long enough to show the gentleman a chair; but, going straight back to his open Bible, he soon forgot the man's presence, and devouring sentence after sentence as a hungry child might devour food, he was heard occasionally to mutter to himself, "Wonderful!" "Wonderful!" while the inner light radiated from every feature of his old face. Our forefathers in America were a Bible-loving, Bible-reading company; almost every day began with what is known as "the family devotions," and they were not even hurried. Now, in ninety-nine homes out of a hundred, they are either spasmodically revived or left to lie in utter neglect.

The time was in England, and that not so far away, when human greatness was often accounted for by Bible study. Men believed themselves to bring from this Book divine wisdom. When a father consulted Earl Cairns as to what books his son should read in his preparation for the law practice, the great Earl answered, "Let him begin with the Bible. There he will find the foundation of all law, as well as all morality." Sir Matthew Hale declared "There is no book like the Bible for learning, wisdom, and justice." Bacon, Blackstone, Lords Littleton and Erskin, Wilberforce and Gladstone,—what great students of the Word they were! And what great souls they developed by steeping them in Scripture! What a strange contrast the present Englishman presents. Dr. G. H. Knight, in a recently published book, says, "An allusion to a Bible story has more than once set half the House of Commons wondering where it came from." If one visited Washington City and mingled with our national lawmakers, and heard them talk on Biblical subjects, he might feel as George Ade. He said, "I hoped to see the day when I would represent the Tenth District in Congress. I have not realized my boyish ambition; but I have seen Congress, and I am reconciled."

## Is the Modern Bible School? 139

It is doubtful whether the English race, once putting aside the Bible, can ever duplicate the great names of the past. Ruskin was a remarkable soul, and the flight of time can all too seldom see his accomplishments repeated; and John Ruskin wrote, "All that I have taught of art, everything that I have been in any thought of mine, whatever I have done in my life, has simply been due to the fact that when I was a child my mother daily read with me a portion of the Bible and daily made me learn a part by heart."

The direst need of the American nation is not a navy nor army; not colleges nor commerce; it is not even a revival of religion, in the common employment of that phrase; but it is a revival of Bible-reading. To be steeped in the sentence of this sacred Book lends an unconquerable strength to any people, insures an intellectual progress that is irresistible, and produces a religious revival that is both deep and far-reaching. When God commanded Joshua to be a builder of a nation, He commenced with him by saying, "This book of the law shall not depart out of thy mouth; but thou shalt meditate therein day and night, that thou mayest observe to do according to all that is written therein: for then thou shalt make thy way prosperous, and then thou shalt have good success."

### The Wander-Lust.

"And they shall wander from sea to sea, and from the north even to the east, and they shall run to and fro to seek the word of the Lord, and shall not find it."

Strange how Scripture can express the relation between strenuous living and spiritual dying; between rapid transit and fading truth.

*Our locomotion has become the enemy of our meditation.*

We shoot from place to place with such rapidity that even reason is upset, and spiritual meditation is made impractical if not impossible. I think I never realized this fact more than recently when in one day I read the reports of the hardship endured fifty years ago by a boy who sought to gain an education, and those being experienced now by the lad mentally ambitious. The first related to A. J. Gordon's college life, when as a lad it was decided he should go to school, and the place of his education was selected. His son writes —"In a suit of clothes made by his mother's

## Is the Modern Bible School? 141

hands from cloth spun in the old mill, he started from home. A long walk truly, thirty-four miles, when one is baggage train as well as infantry. Yet doubtless the bag in which he carried his clothes was not heavily loaded —a change of clothing, a Virgil, and an algebra." "The country through which he passed was especially beautiful, Cardigan and Ragged mountains, round the base of Kearsarge and by Sunapee Lake into the town where the school was situated, in New London." What a beautiful and suggestive description! It must have taken at least two days for the trip. What thoughts would surge through the boy's soul as he climbed the mountain side, descended the valley, and trudged on to college! What meditations would fill the mind, when at night, in some country home he lay in a deep feather bed, and with all the world shut out, faced God and thought about the future. But those days are over. The lad who goes to college now, if he cross the continent, is whirled along on iron wheels; the hum of human voices is in his ears; he simply spends three days in a moving hotel; and if he go a shorter distance, he drives his father's car, and forgets the God above, and overruns the pedestrians below. A recent graduate was asked to tell of the hardships of his early education and he replied, "I lived seven blocks from the Carnegie Library and we had no automobile." "They shall wander from sea to sea and from the north even to the east, they shall run to and fro to seek the word of the Lord, and shall not find it."

*This strenuous living militates against Bible study.*

If only men would stop a while and sit down and open the Book it would speak to them unless they were too tired to give attention to the tale it was telling. Too often, we fear, that is the case. Horace Bushnell said, "My experience is that the Bible is dull when I am dull; when I am really alive the text comes upon me with a tidal wave of living affinity. It opens up discoveries and reveals depths faster than I can make note of them." But when do we get the tidal waves? When do we stop long enough for tidal waves to even overtake us? The race of the century is the ruin of Christianity. In Liverpool one day I went down to the Mersey River. I saw scores of vessels, many of which seemed shipshape; but all of them appeared stranded, or possibly in dry dock. I said to my walking companion, "Why are so many of these vessels dragged into dry dock; are they all in need of repair?" He replied, "No, they are in perfect repair, they are in to be loaded. You see, you do not quite understand. The Mersey River is running out to the ocean now; but tonight the tide will turn and the ocean will come into this river, flooding and filling its every part, and these freighted vessels will be lifted to places of power; and pulling out to sea, will ply their ways to the ends of the earth." In reflecting upon the remark later, I said, It is a parable of spiritual life! The reason so many of us are stranded and cannot go, is that the stream of life is running out. If only we knew how to use the closets of prayer or the curtains of night to find and face God, and let all the fullness of the Godhead flood us, and lift us, we would become vessels of power, and bear to the uttermost parts of the earth the golden truths of the gospel of the Son of God. When the Mersey river runs out to sea it sinks and grows shallow; but when the great sea comes into the river, it rises alike in volume and power. It is a parable! When shall we cease from "running to and fro" long enough to read the Word of the Lord? When shall we know that no professional teaching can ever take the place of the personal perusal? More and more this swiftly traveling, starving crowd are waking up to the fact that many of their journeys are in vain, so far at least as finding at the end of them either spiritual food or drink.

*The non-scriptural minister has produced a Scriptural famine.*

There are people in every city, and their name is legion, who travel from sanctuary to sanctuary, and wander from sea to sea, in search of the truth and never find it. The sanctuary in which they spend the Sabbath does not prove to be like John Hus' "Bethlehem"—"The House of Bread." Many of them are not even respectable lunch counters for the soul. The milk they serve is skimmed indeed, and their philosophical sandwiches have in them no meat of the Word, only a thin spread of science, or philosophy or history. Much of it reminds one of what happened nearly thirty years ago in a notable Church of Minneapolis. Dr. John H. Elliott, my co-laborer, had preached one night and some interested souls had been taken into a side room to be prayed with by personal workers, and the sexton showed some impatience about continuing the lights; whereupon Dr. Elliott thought to engage him in conversation and keep him content until the instruction was finished. After a moment it occurred to him to ask the man if he was a Christian, to which he replied "No." "That is strange," said Elliott, "and you a janitor of a Christian church." "How long have you been in this position?" "About ten years," was the answer. "Well, why are you not a Christian?" "Well," answered the sexton, "I don't exactly know why; no one has ever spoken to me about it." "What!" said Dr. Elliott, "has not the pastor spoken to you about being a Christian in these ten years?" "No" said the sexton, "I don't think Dr. C—— would like to talk on the subject of religion. We talk on a lot of other things but he has never made any mention of that subject." The pathos of the story is that it is a parable with increasing application.

We are sometimes compelled to question whether the Church of God on the whole has been profited by the exchange of a farmer preacher for the seminary output. That man of former days who divided his time between tilling the soil and steeping his soul in Scripture quotations, and Scriptural thought was no mean teacher. At his feet some of us grew up, and we have never ceased to thank God for the fact that, while he talked to us in no terms of science and his very tongue would have halted at the phrase "moral philosophy" he did know the Word of God; he did know the will of the Lord; he did dwell on the "thus saith the Lord," and he did come from a sacred trysting place with the Most High; and he did make the impression that he was God's man, with God's message; and we were mightily moved by it; moved emotionally, moved morally, moved mentally, moved spiritually. We never went to the sanctuary in vain! When asking these fathers for bread, they did not hand us cut a stone of science; or if we asked an egg, they did not for an egg give us the scorpion of philosophy.

I am not asking that the preacher of the twentieth century be as unschooled as was his predecessor in the nineteenth; I am only declaring it is a profound pity that having become more schooled, he has become less Scriptural. I doubt if for him the times can ever even twist, much less change the imperative sentence of Scripture, "Preach the Word!"

## Is the Modern Bible School? 147

John Watson never said a saner thing than when he remarked, "There are enough men to ventilate doubts without the preacher's assistance. From him the world expects faith; and the dynamic of one man, believing with all his mind and all his heart, is incalculable. Doubt can be got anywhere; faith ought to be supplied by the pulpit."

And if the relation of the wander-lust to the Word-famine is evident, then the relation of both to

### The Waiting Youth

is as logical as the connection of Scripture is here close and consecutive. "In that day shall the fair virgins and young men faint for thirst." Is that our day? Let's see—

*Youth is still strongly characterized by spiritual desires and aspirations!*

The young convert comes as close to God now as he ever did. If he be truly regenerated he begins the Christian life with the same emotions which characterized his grandsires, though he has come to express them differently. His disposition to pray is the first proof of the Spirit's work; and the disposition to know what God has spoken is in itself the sign of sonship. As the babe's first word is commonly "Mama" or "Papa," so the new-born soul cries Abba Father, and listens to hear what the Father will say. Some of us who are older, and whose emotional natures like our joints, have become a bit stiff, may have forgotten in part how we used to feel in spirit, as we have also forgotten some of the exuberance of the flesh; but we may be assured that the race changes not and that Christ is "the same yesterday, today, and forever," and that the young men and women who are coming to Him now, are just as restless as we were at their age, and just as anxious to know God as we were at their same point of experience, and just as thirsty for an additional portion of His Word, and for the divine direction of His Spirit as we (who are now in middle life) were when the great soul-decisions of thirty years ago were being made.

If I were a man of the world, and moved only in the social round or commercial realm, and was compelled to face from day to day "the bloodless, worn out society," of which John Watson speaks, I should well nigh lose confidence in all spiritual things. But my soul renews its youth when I stand in the midst of the young men and women now studying in the Northwestern Bible and Missionary Training School, the majority of whom have come away from the farm, none of whom are far removed from the day of their regeneration and consecration, the most of whom are what Gordon once called "the raw material," ready to be hand-made for God. When they pray I am carried on the wings of their petitions into the Divine presence. When they sing I am caught by the exuberance of their spirit and again reach the mountain-top. When they speak I am illumined by the very sparkle of their eyes and the joy of their faces; and in that illumination I see God! Oh, what would be the pathos of the world without youth; and what would be the prospect of the Church without converted children, "Fair virgins and young men thirsting for God!"

*With this company comes the Church's greatest opportunity.*

Let teachers tread lightly here; it is holy ground! And yet, let them speak with alacrity, it is a gracious opportunity. I never look into the faces of this crowd of young men and women, the most of whom were converted but yesterday, many of whom are too well advanced in years to sit down in the grade school with what they would call "the babies," and the most of whom are too poor in purse to attempt the select school of secondary grade, but I thank God for the privilege of teaching them; and I never look into their intelligent faces and mark the perfectly marvelous progress they make from week to week, without feeling a contempt for those people who can never be interested in any section of society save the upper-crust! They are like the priests and Pharisees of Christ's day, who, when the officers sent to arrest Him, returned, saying, "Never man spake like this man," answered "Are ye also deceived? Have any of the rulers believed on him?"

The longer I live the less I am concerned about the opinion of the ruling classes, for I know that this raw material, if rightly educated and trained for God, will, with the true Ruler, reign tomorrow. Society is in eternal revolution. It is a depressing thing to see the top go down to the bottom. But, oh, to watch the other side! What an inspiration to see the bottom come to the top! And may I remind you that there is but one thing that can lift it, and that is the religion of Christ expressed in the sacred Scriptures.

What then is the greatest spiritual movement of the century? You will dissent, I have no doubt; but I speak from the deepest conviction.

*The modern Bible Conference, and the Bible and Missionary Training School.*

The first is a short course in Scripture; the second, a more complete training in the same. In them God has flung His lines of defense from sea to sea; and destructive criticism— the enemy that has come in like a flood—is finding the Bible Conference and the Bible School capable of both stubborn and successful resistance. Every state in the Union has its Bible Conference in multiplied numbers. Thirty years ago Northfield stood almost alone in America, and Keswick was well nigh solitary in England; and thirty years ago the Moody Institute was a solitary little sister, and looked upon with scorn by the mature and proud-pursed schools of the land; and Spurgeon's College was held in disdain by Doctors of Divinity! But that God was in the movement can hardly be disputed when we recall the names of the Bible Conference and Bible School advocates—Spurgeon, Guinness, Meyer, Morgan and others of the Old World;

Moody, Gordon, Simpson, White, Torrey, Gray, Frost and other like men in the New World.

These Conferences and Schools are not the exponents of science, not the special advocates of philosophy, not the instructors in history. It is an age of specializing, and they have deliberately chosen to specialize in the knowledge of God's Word. Tens and hundreds of thousands of ministers and laymen attend upon these conferences every summer, and Keswick in England, Northfield and Winona in America are now names that suggest two things—the study of the Word of God, and the deepening of the spiritual life; and the Bible schools established in New York, South Nyack, Philadelphia, Chicago, Minneapolis, Los Angeles, and other cities, are making greater strides, everything considered, than any class of schools that have ever sprung into existence. They have been the subjects of constant criticism, the objects of repeated ridicule. They have been characterized as "educational short-cuts;" their graduates have been spoken of as "unscholarly" and "crude;" but perhaps Dr. Gordon's reply is significant, "I prefer a little man with a great gospel to a great man with a little gospel!"

Ours is a great gospel! The people that best proclaim it are marked for progress; and those that most deny it are destined to perish.

## CHAPTER VII.

## IS A CONFEDERACY OF CONSERVATIVES THE CALL OF THE HOUR?

### Isa. 8:11-20.

"For the Lord spake thus to me with a strong hand, and instructed me that I should not walk in the way of this people, saying, Say ye not, A confederacy, to all them to whom this people shall say, A confederacy; neither fear ye their fear, nor be afraid. Sanctify the Lord of hosts himself; and let him be your fear, and let him be your dread. And he shall be for a sanctuary; but for a stone of stumbling and for a rock of offence to both the houses of Israel, for a gin and for a snare to the inhabitants of Jerusalem. And many among them shall stumble, and fall, and be broken, and be snared, and be taken. Bind up the testimony, seal the law among my disciples. And I will wait upon the Lord, that hideth his face from the house of Jacob, and I will look for him. Behold, I and the children whom the Lord hath given me are for signs and for wonders in Israel from the Lord of hosts, which dwelleth in mount Zion. And when they shall say unto you, Seek unto them that have familiar spirits, and unto wizards that peep, and that mutter: should not a people seek unto their God? for the living to the dead? To the law and to the testimony: if they speak not according to this word, it is because there is no light in them."

## Is a Confederacy the Call?

*For twenty centuries the visible Church of Christ has travelled by a path characterized by many curves. Some of these have been sharp and even striking, and good men have wondered what the new direction meant. Today that institution stands before diverging paths and is compelled, therefore, to debate which way she shall take, for it is manifestly evident that these paths can never have a common termination; for, Christianity, rightly defined, has come to the crisis of its existence, and its entire future rests with the decision which must at once be made.

The parallelism between Judah and the hour of our text, and Christianity and the hour to which we have come, is at once wonderful and striking. Then there was an unnatural combination of Israel with Syrian foreigners against Judah, and the national theocracy was threatened to the point where the Prophet pointed to God as the only and yet adequate hope. He realized, however, and clearly voiced his conviction, that their salvation from the Lord depended upon their repudiation of a popular confederacy, and their creation of a

* This chapter is in pamphlet form, published by "The Book Stall," 113 Fulton St., N. Y. City. Herbert Booth's book on this same subject is a classic.

confederacy of their own, the inspiring spirit of which should be none other than "the Lord of hosts" Himself.

The parallelism with the present-day predicament is perfect, and the call of the hour is

A CHRISTIAN CONFEDERACY.

Let me hasten at once to define the phrase! "The Christian confederacy," as it lies in my mind, is a close fellowship, yea, even an organization, of true and evangelical conservatives; or, if you please, of those men and women, churches, schools, and other Christian institutions, that are willing to take the exact position adopted by Martin Luther when he began his reformation, namely that the Bible is 'the very Word of God, and is, therefore, and must forever remain, the only rule of faith and practice. The time has fully come for both energetic and persistent propagation of the "faith once delivered" as the only antidote to that infidelity which has forced its way beyond the very altars of our churches, and is sliming our schools with its deadly saliva. The unmistakable sign of such a confederacy to come exists in the circumstance that within two or three years, God, by the still small voice of His Spirit, has spoken to great Christian

## Is a Confederacy the Call? 157

leaders in different portions of the great civilized world, upon this subject; and, as they have met in national and international conferences for exchange of thought and feeling, they have again and again stood amazed to discover with what unanimity the Spirit had spoken to individuals—separated by great distances, by denominational names, and even by distinct tongues. It is another illustration of God's own method of making known His will. To the men who have had ears to hear, there has been a voice behind them saying, "This is the way, walk ye in it." To the conservative prophets of our day God is saying again what He said to Isaiah, and through Isaiah, to Israel, "Say ye not, A confederacy, etc." (vss. 12-20).

How marvelously this portion of scripture compasses the conception already stated. Such a confederacy as is mentioned here is already in existence, and we are enjoined by the Lord not to accept and adopt it.

Its name is

"THE FEDERAL COUNCIL

of the Churches of Christ in America."

It professes to represent more than thirty denominations, it claims to have a co-operative membership of more than seventeen millions.

Its pretentions and appeal while having no such proportions have undoubtedly met with a great and popular response. The bases of this response may be easily discovered. They lie in three things.

It proposes a close interdenominational co-operation; it promises unification of sentiment by a common service; and, it has chosen, as its prominent leaders, special exponents of liberal theology. In each of these facts, it represents the spirit of the times to which we belong.

*It proposes a close interdenominational co-operation.*

That proposition is expressed in its very name—"The Federal Council of the Churches of Christ in America." It does not limit its fellowship by any exclusive terms. While it has denied Unitarians representation, it was not so much on the ground of doctrine as in the circumstance of a name. Unitarians have never professed to be "Churches of Christ" even by the most far-fetched of definitions.

As early as 1912 the "Council" claimed duly appointed delegates from thirty-two denominations. The very number of denominations mentioned shows how attenuated is the defini-

## Is a Confederacy the Call? 159

tion,—"Churches of Christ." The prominent word therefore, is not Christianity; it is "consolidation" instead,—one of the most popular words of the age to which we belong.

That word was employed first of all in the economic field, and in the interest of commercial advantages; and there it has been so eminently successful that competition is more and more fading from trade, and mergers,—known as monopolies—more and more control.

Certain men, looked upon by some as great religious leaders, have called attention to this advantage in the economic world, have reminded their auditors and readers that this accrues alike to the monopolist and to the people, and have boldly argued that the churches of the land ought to learn from "the children of this generation, who are wiser in their day and generation than the children of light;" and that mergers and Christian corporations ought to kill out the denominational competition which has resulted alike in over-churched villages and no-church communities. It is the dream of a great unification!

This "Federal Council" conception contains features of advantage not to be ignored or despised by any thoughtful man. Beyond all question the bitter denominational debates over minor points, while sometimes resulting in clearer convictions as to Scripture teaching, more often produced anger, wrath, malice, prejudices—anti-Christian results!

Beyond all doubt, Christ intended that there should be place for the play of individual opinions in the interpretation alike of the Scriptures and Himself; and yet hoped that those who might not see eye to eye on other subjects, would ignore their minor differences and unite upon the major bases of their belief.

Again, it is clear that co-operation has advantages in both spirit and method over competition; and that where one man might chase a thousand, two, if united, might put ten thousand to flight. How often has the human chain saved men, just because six or a dozen or twenty men, joined hands and flinging the line out into the surf to the point where the deepest wader, might lay hands upon the endangered or drowning one, and, by a pull all together, bring him to shore.

Men have seen these things so clearly, and realized them with such increasing interest, that the call for a closer denomination affiliation has met the instant response of great masses of church members; and this confederacy has been the easy result.

*Furthermore, it promises unification of sentiment by a common service.*

The language of its present President is: "Christian efficiency lies not in the effort to get everybody to agree about everything, but in the effort to free the world of sin." It is such a sentiment as excites popular applause! There are so many things wrong in the world that need righting, that leaders in religion and reform can scarcely afford to despise profferred help, particularly if it be offered by good men and they be animated by righteous motives! Their interests are so far identical in character—in matters for instance of sanitation, in the necessity of education, in the improvement of environment, in social needs, and opportunities of social service, that the appeal of co-operation, whenever and wherever possible, strikes the most popular of all cords, and men are reminded of the fact, (and it is a fact)—that the more they work together, the better they understand one another; and, that such increasing acquaintance and fellowship of service crucifies needless prejudices and quickens into life mutual appreciations.

That truth is illustrated by every factory and shop in the land. Men of different nationalities, different tongues, different opinions, different sentiments,—working side by side, at common tasks, become a sort of brotherhood; and are much less likely to fight among themselves than they are to scrap with the fellows from the factory across the way.

The leaders of "the Federal Council" have seen this and have said, "Let's not debate over our differences; but rather, undertake together common tasks, and our unity of feeling and opinion will necessarily be fostered by our agreement in action."

*Its prominent leaders are exponents of liberal theology.*

The truth of this is put past all dispute by merely calling attention to their names, and reviewing their so-called theological writings. If, by anyone it is denied, the denial would only be in the interest of maintaining the unity for which it stands; and when our attention is called to the names of known conservatives who occupy prominent places, a little study discovers the fact that in every instance they occupy a secondary place, and have been elect-

## Is a Confederacy the Call? 163

ed to that, in the hope of keeping in line with this movement, radical conservatives.

This liberal leadership is not condemnable, viewed from the standpoint of the Federal Council. The very effort to unite all parties in the present-day denominations makes necessary some recognition of theological conservatives, and equally necessary the leadership of liberals. Conservatism always tends to exclusiveness; Liberalism always manifests toleration; and the very life of such a movement as "the Federal Council" depends upon toleration. And yet, to prove that toleration is not carried to the point where Christ can be utterly put aside, Unitarians were denied representation in this movement. It thereby keeps the semblance of consistency in the name "The Federal Council of *Churches of Christ* in America."

Why then, is not the Council sufficient? Why should the Lord be supposed to be speaking to certain men, insisting that they should not walk in the way of this people, saying "Say not ye, A confederacy, to all them to whom this people shall say, A confederacy; neither fear their fear, nor be afraid"—speaking to the great leaders in Europe, in England, and in Canada, in the East; in the South, and in the Southwest, in the Northwest, and in the center of the land saying "Sanctify the Lord of hosts himself: and let him be your fear, and let him be your dread. And he shall be for a sanctuary; but for a stone of stumbling and for a rock of offence to both the houses of Israel, for a gin and for a snare to the inhabitants of Jerusalem. And many among them shall stumble, and fall, and be broken, and be snared and be taken. Bind up the testimony, seal the law among my disciples," advising a definite movement which Herbert Booth has in his book well and wisely named

"THE CHRISTIAN CONFEDERACY!"

What would be the essential difference between such a confederacy and the Federal Council? And what would be the advantages, if any, in the latter as against the former? And what could possibly be the justification of a new movement, at a time when religious movements are already confessedly over-multiplied?

Let us understand first of all:—

*Its very birth must come of unity in Biblical faith.* The men who have thought about such a movement, and who have conferred together about its inauguration, and who now have in

## Is a Confederacy the Call?

mind the calling of a great convention that shall represent alike a mighty constituency of the Old and New World, are one in their unshaken faith that "the Bible is the very Word of God," and "Christ is the very Son of God," and "the cross the only way of salvation." Think of our Saviour's prayer concerning His disciples, and in the name of the proper exegesis, omit not its main point—"That they all may be one; as thou, Father, art in me, and I in thee, that they also may be one in us." To what end? That they might be unified in endeavor? No!; that they might cease from bickerings and debates? No!; that they might undertake the task of cleaning up a nasty world? No!; that they might even join hands in the endeavor to save men from sin? No! But "THAT THE WORLD MAY BELIEVE THAT THOU HAST SENT ME." There is no sentence possible to human thought or speech that could more clearly express at once the authority of the Bible, the deity of Christ, and the philosophy of the divine plan of salvation, than does that sentiment; and the people *"who are one"* in these things, scattered through the different denominations, are today the absolute answer of God to the prayer of His Son.

It was after A. J. F. Behrends came back

to the faith from which he had temporarily drifted, that he said: "The angel of unity is our pillar of cloud and fire, and always has been; and we knew it not. We ache and pray for that which has already come. Can it be that our Lord's prayer has remained unanswered, all these centuries? For myself, at least, the years have taught me, that we need to say 'we are one,' as well as to pray that we may be one. I have learned that the unities of the Christian faith are more mighty and majestic than the differences. I have grasped the hand of many a Catholic layman and priest, when at the clasp of palms and mutual greetings the yawning chasm vanished."

Certainly! The man who is in the Catholic Church, but has the experience of the grace of God, (as some of them have unquestionably had,) entertains an unshaken confidence in the Bible, seeking thereby to conform his conduct and form his character, who accepts Jesus Christ as the very Son of God, and His sufferings on Calvary as the atonement for his sin, is a thousand fold more my brother than the man who belongs to my denomination in name, but in fact repudiates all of these fundamentals of the Christian faith. The time has come, in the Northland at least, when it

## Is a Confederacy the Call?

makes a thousand fold less difference to many of us as to the denominational label than it does as to the doctrinal life. We know that two men, belonging to different denominations, may hold identical bases, and we know that two belonging to the same denomination, and that, evangelical in name, are, again and again, as remote apart as the Unitarian and Trinitarian, as far removed from one another in convictions, and conceptions as the skeptic is removed from the believer; and sometimes as remote as the atheist is from the Christian. Think of the incongruity of calling I. M. Haldeman and Geo. Burman Foster both Baptists: of naming Reginald Campbell and Campbell Morgan both Congregationalists; labeling L. W. Munhall and the late Professor Terry both Methodists, of defining Ex-President Patten and President Francis Brown as alike Presbyterians! Has the sentence of the Old Testament lost its significance entirely—"Can two walk together except they be agreed?" Has the symbolism of Deuteronomy no longer any spiritual significance—"Thou shalt not plow with the ox and the ass together?" Is there no longer any typical truth in the command "Thou shalt not wear a garment of divers sorts, as of woolen and linen?" Can we afford, just because we fling over it the name "Christian" for a covering, the philosophy of an Ingersoll, and say, "You have your opinion and I have mine, let it go! Let's join hands and be good fellows?" Is John's (II Jno. 2: 9-11) injunction not to receive the rejector of Christ out of date? Has the day arrived when Jude's "certain men, crept in unawares" instead of being now condemned as ministers of the devil, because they preach a bloodless righteousness, denying the very Christ that bought them, are to be called "brothers;" and, are we to labor together when a part of our company reject the Scriptures, repudiate the virgin birth, excoriate the claims of the supernatural, and bring the God of the Old Testament to the level of a tribal deity, and the God of the New to that of a Jewish bastard? Has the hour arrived when men who are "in Israel, but not of her," (in the Church, but not of Christ) can form an alliance with her enemies and the true worshiper give his consent to the compact?

Should the world marvel, when such a confederacy is attempted, that God should speak to certain men, saying, "Walk not in the way of this people; join not a confederacy of this kind! Sanctify the Lord of hosts, himself,

## Is a Confederacy the Call? 169

and let him be your fear." Has the time come when Truth is tolerant and willing to compromise with error, when light "should enter into communion" with darkness; and "righteousness" into "fellowship with unrighteousness," and "believers" should voluntarily yoke themselves "with unbelievers," and Christ come into concord with Belial, and the "disciples" join hands "with the infidels," *in service* (II Tim. 4:1)?

Without at all attempting to name individuals, but standing upon the broad plain of what so-called religious leaders have themselves professed and put into print, there are scores of us, who believe that the Word of the Lord—"Come ye out from among them, and be ye separate" looks to another "confederacy" altogether, namely, a confederacy in Biblical faith; to a better brotherhood,—namely one that shall seek to let the world know that God—according to the authority of the Scriptures—sent His only begotten Son,—Christ, and if we are not "one in Him" we are not one at all!

Truly the time has come for the re-affirmation of the Apostle's Creed, and the fellowship that follows the same: "I believe in God the Father Almighty; and in Jesus Christ, His only Son, our Lord, begotten before all worlds, the very God of very God, who for us came down from heaven and was conceived of the Virgin Mary by the Holy Ghost." And the only church that is worthy to wear His name must be "that holy church throughout all the world which does acknowledge the Father, of infinite majesty, His true and only Son, and the Holy Ghost, the Comforter."

*The value of such a confederacy would depend upon its loyalty to Biblical precepts.*

The time has come when the so-called Christian church is somewhat equally distributed among the advocates of an infallible Consciousness, an infallible Church, and an infallible Book. No one contends that all of these are infallible; and that to believe any one of them is sufficient in the sight of God; while to believe in them all is an additional merit! On the other hand, they have created partitions in the Church of Christ, far more positive than any ever known as denominational barriers! Just as Rome, by adopting an "Infallible Church," repudiated the infallibility of the Book, so liberal theology, in adopting an "infallible Consciousness" compels the Book to step aside when that Con-

## Is a Confederacy the Call?

sciousness and Revelation are in apparent conflict. The repudiation of Revelation by Rome, and the adoption of the "Infallible Church" resulted in the Traditionalism that accounts for the Dark Ages; but the adoption of an "inner religious consciousness" as against an external revelation, has resulted in Rationalism and Materialism which increasingly read God out of His own universe and has flung the world into the horrors of a hellish war!

The true Christian confederacy will make its every appeal to the exact source to which Christ turned in defense alike of teaching and conduct, namely—the Sacred Scriptures; and insist that not only creeds and opinions be corrected thereby, but our conduct as well. The heresy of modern times is no more in theological thinking than it is in individual living! As Herbert Booth has remarked, "It is not sufficient to rally around a standard of doctrine only. False doctrine is not the sole cause of the Church's stagnation and defeat; it is not even the chief cause! Her worldliness, self-indulgence and backsliding are even more potent reasons." And only a Confederacy that does call professed Christians unto more righteous living, as well as to more correct thinking, will accomplish aught for the world.

However, never let it be forgotten that "as a man thinketh in his heart so is he!" Sound teaching is absolutely essential to sound practice. The relation between the two is that of cause and effect; and if such a confederacy as Booth has named, and scores of our greatest teachers have dreamed and desired is now to be inaugurated, it must mean for ministers of the gospel and for laymen alike, a call to higher living, to a course of conduct that will honor Christ, that will exalt the spiritual and repudiate the sensual, that will not invite criticism from the world, but, rather, set before it an example upon which Christ could put His approval, and into which He will dare to put His Holy Spirit.

*The rapidity of its growth will rest with the affiliation of covenant-forces.*

By covenant-forces I mean such individuals and organizations as will be ready to enter into such a covenant as would concede forever the question of the authority of the Scriptures, the deity of Christ, the personality and power of the Holy Spirit, salvation by the

## Is a Confederacy the Call? 173

atonement, separateness from the world, the consecration of self to the cause of Jesus Christ, an acceptation of the Scriptural second coming of the Lord; and, a confederacy with others, to bear our witness, in this generation, to all the nations of the earth.

For such an affiliation, or confederacy, we have numerous individuals and organizations ready and waiting. Hundreds of the most eminent preachers of the world (and as yet the world's most eminent preachers are its most conservative thinkers) made up of the very men who believe in a stand for the things afore mentioned, should link their hands and recognize the answer to their Lord's prayer, namely that they are essentially one. Within a few years as we have said in the previous chapter there have sprung up in America and the Old World multitudes of Bible conferences! Almost without exception these are conducted by the very men whose unity of faith is the marvel of the hour. They should be related, become a chain with which our God could join together the evangelical forces of the land.

In this same period, Bible Training Schools have started up to speak the shibboleth of the Scripture, and to turn back the wave of skepticism created by the very breath of those theological seminaries that have adopted so-called "Modernism." And, to these individual leaders and these mighty and increasing instructors, should be added the Lord's "little flock" out of every church, whose confidence in the Bible and in Christ, has remained unshaken!

When such a fellowship is created, and when the hands of such men are linked, and such instructors are correlated, the tide of criticism, largely German in origin, will find that it has met a more stubborn resistance than German soldiers have met at Verdun. Some of us believe that such a movement is as sure as God lives; and that before it the infidelity which has characterized, divided and cursed our churches, is destined to constant warfare, if not an ignominious defeat.

Out of this Christian Confederacy must come an educational process that will reach to the uttermost parts of the earth! Text books for the use of colleges and Bible Schools must be provided, and conservative literature that shall be used to the ends of the earth should come from the same. It is nothing less than intolerable to longer consent to liberalism in our Sunday School instruction. The whole

## Is a Confederacy the Call?   175

subject of evangelism should be clearly presented and only evangelists who know the evangel tolerated in our believing bodies; and with this movement evangelism itself should be forever linked with that social service which is not born of "the modern's" philosophy, but is the very breath of the Christian religion, and will be rendered not in the power of man's invention, but in the demonstration of the Spirit.

What then, is the conclusion, save

### THE CALL OF THE CROSS.

*It is a call to consecration for the professing Christian.*

There has never been an hour when that call was as loud as now. The boasted "brotherhood of man" has broken down, and all over Europe, and in parts of Asia, and in great sections of the American continent, battle and blood tramples "brotherhood" under unholy feet. And yet men learn so slowly that all over America we are adopting now the very philosophy (Militarism) exploited in Germany, France and England for the betterment, and even the salvation of men! It is all in vain, apart from Him whose name we bear, to whom alone we owe our first, last, and eternal allegiance. In the language of Henry Mabie, "We are not to stop short of complete crucifixion of everything that stands between us and obedience to His will." The Pauline confession is the idea for us, "I have been crucified with Christ, and it is no longer I that live; but Christ liveth in me, and that life which I now live in the flesh, I live in the faith which is in the Son of God who loved me and gave himself up for me." If in the language of the great French preacher Lacordaire, "The church was born crucified" then the weakness of the hour may be due to the circumstance that we have healed the wound, and how else can we break it than by a crucifixion of the flesh of the individual who enters into this membership—such a crucifixion as would fill up that which is left of the sufferings of Christ.

The language of Father Ryan is apropos—

"Our dim eyes ask a beacon, and our weary feet a
  guide,
 And our hearts of all life's mysteries seek the
  meaning and the key;
 And a cross gleams o'er our pathway, on it hangs
  the Crucified,
 And He answers all our yearnings by the whisper
  'Follow Me.'"

## Is a Confederacy the Call? 177

*It is a call to reformation for the professing Church.*

Mark you, I employ the phrase "the professing Church" knowing full well that there is a profession in the Churches to which there is no corresponding possession. To be sure, we need again the Spirit of a Luther to declare the truth of God's Word, "The just shall live by faith;" but we need, none the less, the return of Carey's spirit to put our convictions into action; for much of the church, reformation is not sufficient; regeneration is needed rather; but for practically all of it, reformation.

In the judgment of some of us the professing church has not only grown great branches but developed certain leaves under the shadow of which "fowls of the air" have indeed taken refuge in the form of University and College presidents, liberal pastors, theological professors, instructors in biology, geology, paleontology, philosophy and related themes,—who prove their loyalty to "the prince of the power of the air," by their scoffs at Scripture, their rejection of Jesus, their insistence upon Darwinism, their exaltation of man! It is not at all certain that these branches can be cut away or the occupants of the church tree dislodged from their comfortable perches, but it is clear that the children of the King can give to the world an exhibition of a truer church within the church, and preach the Word of life in the power of the same Spirit who came upon Peter at Pentecost, and endowed Paul in the old days! Truly, in the language of Sir Robert Anderson, "It is essential now to distinguish between the 'Church' as a society the administration of which was entrusted to men on earth, and the 'Church' as the body of Christ, dependent only upon Himself as its Lord and head." And, we ought to enhearten ourselves with the thought that the building up of "the Church, which is his body," is His own work, and that it cannot fail. "The gates of hell" have prevailed against the organized Society, "the outward frame," as Alford calls it, and is pushing it more and more to the point of apostasy—foretold in Scripture.

But there is a Church within the church, against which those gates will not, and cannot prevail—the true body of Christ. To attempt to name that body would be at once foolish, and, in the judgment of the world (in the church and out of the church), would be an egoism and an assumption,—equally condemn-

## Is a Confederacy the Call?

able. No man knows! But we believe that the exaltation of the name of Christ will result in a demonstration of the true Church, and that there will gather to the standard that exalts "His name above every name," the true men and women of God throughout the length and breadth of the land; and that *that* "confederacy" will increasingly correspond to "the Church, which is his body." It ought not to be forgotten that the word "Eagle" is the Old Testament typical word for saint, and that in speaking of Christ, it is said that "where the body is thither will the eagles be gathered together."

Finally, *It is a call to world-evangelization in this generation.*

There never was a more futile hope than that which men are now urging in a multitude of ministries. Like the host that went forth in Gideon's day, they are too many! Too many by all those that bend not the knee acknowledging the deity of Christ; too many by all those that drink not from the wells of salvation; (the Word) too many by all those that scorn the efficiency of the shed blood!

If every foreign missionary who denies the authority of the Book, the virgin birth, the

Biblical report of the supernatural—involving all miracle working, the resurrection of Christ included—were dismissed from service at once, we would be instantly nearer the discharge of our province of preaching this "gospel of the kingdom in all the world for a witness." They that "preach another gospel" are not aiding in the Great Commission; and Paul tells us, in no uncertain speech, that such as are removing from Him that called them unto the grace of Christ, were "preaching another gospel," and though they be *"angels from heaven,"* are not under blessing, but rather, under curse. The very life of the Commission depends upon elimination from among the commissioned, of both the skeptics and critics. Paradoxical as it may sound, there is a decrease that looks to multiplication. When in the old day certain ones went "out" from the church because "they were not of it," the Church was not weaker but stronger! The gospel went forward with greater rapidity after the apostate Demas had ceased to speak than it ever could have, had he continued.

It remains now, as it ever has, for the Church within the church, to realize the responsibility of world evangelism. In the

## Is a Confederacy the Call?  181

language of A. J. F. Behrends, "The missionary spirit is its beating heart, and animating breath. The lifted Christ is the adequate magnet to draw diverging lines together, and cement His followers not only into a unity of feeling, but into a magnanimity of endeavor, making possible this testimony in all nations in this generation."

The Call of the cross is the Call of the Christ, and as we look into the faces of the rising youth of our churches the call becomes a command—"Pray!" We must pray for men who believe God; who receive His Word; who trust His only begotten Son; who are brothers in Christ because supernaturally begotten, and in whose brotherhood is the only hope of either the true church or the sinning, sinking world!

# What The War Teaches
# or
# The Greatest Lessons of 1917

### R. A. TORREY
**Dean of Bible Institute of Los Angeles**

Price 5c each; 50c dozen.

THE BIOLA BOOK ROOM
Bible Institute of Los Angeles
536-558 South Hope Street
Los Angeles, California.

Copyright 1918
By R. A. Torrey

# THE GREATEST LESSONS OF 1917

"We must work the works of Him that sent me, while it is day: the night cometh, when no man can work." John 9:4.

Our subject is, "The Greatest Lessons of 1917." You will find the text in John 9:4, "We must work the works of Him that sent me, while it is day: the night cometh, when no man can work." You may not see at first the connection between the subject and the text, but you will as we go on, and especially as we close. The year that is just ending is the most momentous that any man now living has ever seen. There is reason to suppose that 1918 will be still more momentous, but that still lies in the future, about which it is not very safe to speculate. The day in which we are living is the day of the largest opportunity and loudest call to unstinted self-sacrifice and untiring service. I would rather live today than any day of this old world's history. Every year has its lessons, but no other year is so rich in lessons as this.

## I. THAT THE BIBLE IS THE WORD OF GOD.

The first great lesson that 1917 teaches is that the Bible is the Word of God.

There has always been abundant proof that the Bible is the Word of God, but the occurrences of the present year give fresh, up-to-date illustration and proof that it is so. The year 1917 proves that the Bible is the Word of God in three ways:

1. First of all, the year 1917 proves the Bible to be the Word of God by fulfilling its prophecies. Fulfilled prophecy is conclusive proof that the Bible is the Word of God. Any book that has the power of looking centuries into the future and predicting with minuteness, precision and accuracy of time person, place and circumstance, events to occur centuries later, must have for its Author the only Being in the universe that knows the end from the beginning, that is, God. Three lines of prophecy have been particularly fulfilled this year:

(1) First, prophecies about the Jews. There are two lines of prophecy concerning the Jews that have been fulfilled in a striking way during the past

year. In the first place, prophecies regarding the sufferings to come upon the Jews in consequence of their disobedience to the revealed will of God as given through Moses. In Deut. 28:37, 41, 47, 48, 58, 59, 64-67 we read, "And thou shalt become an astonishment, a proverb, and a by-word, among all the peoples whither Jehovah shall lead thee away. . . . Thou shalt beget sons and daughters, but they shall not be thine; for they shall go into captivity. . . . Because thou servdst not Jehovah thy God with joyfulness, and with gladness of heart, by reason of the abundance of all things; therefore shalt thou serve thine enemies that Jehovah shall send against thee, in hunger, and in thirst, and in nakedness, and in want of all things; and he shall put a yoke of iron upon thy neck, until he have destroyed thee. . . . If thou wilt not observe to do all the words of this law that are written in this book, that thou mayest fear this glorious and fearful name, JEHOVAH THY GOD; then Jehovah will make thy plagues wonderful, and the plagues of thy seed, even great plagues and of long continuance, and sore sicknesses, and of long continuance. . . . And Jehovah will scatter thee among all peoples, from the one end of the earth even unto the other end of the earth; and there thou shalt serve other gods, which thou hast not known, thou nor thy fathers, even wood and stone. And among these nations shalt thou find no ease, and there shall be no rest for the sole of thy foot; but Jehovah will give thee there a trembling heart, and failing of eyes, and pining of soul; and thy life shall hang in doubt before thee; and thou shalt fear night and day, and shalt have no assurance of thy life. In the morning thou shalt say, Would it were even, and at even thou shalt say, Would it were morning; for the fear of thy heart which thou shalt fear, and for the sight of thine eyes which thou shalt see." These predictions made so many thousand years ago, have been in the process of fulfillment for centuries, but never have they been so remarkably fulfilled as during the past year, notably among the Jews in Poland, but also in other lands. In the second place, a second line of prophecies concerning the Jews have been fulfilled in a notable manner in 1917, namely, prophecies concerning the returning fullness of blessing and glory that is to come to Israel, and their return to their native land. These promises of future glory for Israel have for centuries seemed impossible of fulfillment, but today we see them in course of fulfillment before our very eyes. This is indicated in two ways: first, by the place the Jew now occupies in the government of nations. There is not time to go into this in detail, but if there were it could be shown that to an amazing extent the leading men in the control of the government and commerce and international relations of England and France and Germany are Jews. The man who stands at the forefront in Russia at the present time, Trotzky, is a Jew. A Russian friend who left Petrograd Nov. 29th and who is well informed told me today that there are forty men who really rule there, and that thirty of these forty are Jews though they have taken Russian names. The Jew will have much to say about the settlement of the present war. In addition to this, we have the recent capture of Jerusalem by the English forces, and England's declaration that Jerusalem is to be turned over to the Jews. In such things as these there is the clearest indication that we are well on the way toward the fulfillment of the seemingly incredible prophecies of the Bible regarding the future glory of the Jew, when "the times of the Gentiles" shall have ended. For centuries Jerusalem has been trodden down of the nations (that is, the Gentile nations), as the Lord Jesus predicted it would be (Luke 21:24); and now that "the times of the Gentiles" are near their fulfillment Jerusalem is apparently about to pass from the Gentiles back to the Jew, as our Lord predicted it would (Luke 21:24).

(2) A second class of prophecies has been fulfilled in a remarkable way during the year that is just ending, and that is prophecies concerning war. The Bible declares that in the last days of this dispensation there shall be a multiplying of wars. Our Lord said, "And ye shall hear of wars and rumors of wars; see that ye be not troubled; for these things must needs come to pass; but the end is not yet. For nation shall rise against nation, and king-

dom against kingdom; and there shall be famines and earthquakes in divers places. But all these things are the beginning of travail." (Matt. 24:6-8. See also Jer. 25:26-33.) And God declared through the prophet Daniel, in Dan. 9:26, that "Even unto the end (i. e., the end of this dispensation) shall be war." A short time ago these prophecies seemed impossible of fulfillment. Our wise men, our philosophers and our statesmen said that a great war was an impossibility. We had our Hague Conferences, and built our Peace Palaces, and on the very day of the outbreak of the war, the representatives of different nations were gathering at Geneva for a Peace Conference. Any one who dared to say that the most awful war in the world's history was coming was regarded as a crank and a fanatic. A few years ago, before the outbreak of the present war, The Christian Herald wrote to me and to different persons in this country and across the water, asking our opinion about these Peace Movements, and whether we thought that there ever could be another great war. In answer to this letter of inquiry, I wrote that I was in favor of anything that made for peace even temporarily, but that as far as there never being another great war was concerned, I knew my Bible too well not to know that there could not be permanent peace, but that there was ahead of us the most awful war in all the world's history. Many regarded me as a crank for this statement of opinion, but where are we today?

(3) There is a third class of prophecies in process of fulfillment this year, that is, prophecies concerning the last days. We read in 2 Tim. 3:1-5, "But know this, that *in the last days* grievous times shall come. For men shall be *lovers of self, lovers of money, boastful, haughty, railers, disobedient to parents,* unthankful, unholy; without natural affection, *implacable* (or, trucebreakers), *slanderers,* without self-control, fierce, no lovers of good, *traitors,* headstrong, *puffed up,* lovers of pleasure rather than lovers of God; *holding a form of godliness* (Gott mit uns), but *having denied* the *power thereof."* Until comparatively recently, social philosophers, theologians and popular preachers had persuaded themselves, and sought to persuade us, that we were

hurrying at express rate toward a millennium of universal peace, righteousness and love. Any one who ventured to point to the plain predictions of God's Word regarding "the last days" was regarded as belonging "to a second-class school of religious fanatics." But what has been the history of 1917? It is pictured exactly in these ignored or despised words of Paul which I have just read. If this year 1917 had sat before the camera it could not have been more accurately photographed than it is here in God's camera.

2. The year 1917 proves the Bible to be the Word of God in a second way, that is, by illustrating and confirming its teachings. The teachings of the Bible that have been illustrated and confirmed this year are very many. I will call your attention to but three. First of all, 1 John 2:17, "And the world passeth away, and the lust thereof; but he that doeth the will of God abideth forever." Every year for centuries has been a confirmation of this verse, but never has the transitory character of this present world been more wonderfully illustrated than in the year 1917, when dynasties are changing, thrones are tottering, forms of government are crumbling and dissolving, fortunes are vanishing, reputations are going, and all earthly things are passing away in a most astounding manner. Second, Jer. 17:5, "Thus saith Jehovah: Cursed is the man that trusteth in man, and maketh flesh his arm, and whose heart departeth from Jehovah." We have been trusting in man, putting our confidence in the arm of flesh; we have depended upon our great statesmen, our great philosophers, our great scientists, and our great soldiers. We have departed from God; we have ignored Him in our plans. When I say "we" I mean not only America, but all the nations of the earth. And the arm of flesh has failed us; the unexpected has happened, time and time again. Ruin has overtaken all nations. Men have been wondering why God did not stop the war. If men choose to put their trust in one another instead of in Him, why should He not in His infinite wisdom and righteousness let men drink to the dregs the bitter cup which they have mixed for themselves? It is but a fulfillment of His own Word. In the third place,

the year 1917 has wonderfully illustrated and confirmed the teaching of the Word of God regarding the essential total depravity of man at his best natural estate. The Bible teaching that man, until born again, is at enmity with God (Rom. 8:7), that his will is perverse, his affections corrupt, and his mind blinded, has been much doubted in recent years, it has been held to be a false representation of human nature, but the events of 1917 make it as clear as day that it is an exact picture of man as he is without God. The year has brought clearly to light what rulers and people are at heart, and what has been brought to light is in exact accordance with the teaching of the Bible.

3. The year 1917 has proved the Bible to be the Word of God in a third way, that is by the way in which the Bible meets present day needs, the deepest needs of men and women in this year of our Lord 1917. To what book shall we go in such strange and trying days as these are? There is but one book to which we can go. Last Monday there was a striking editorial in the Los Angeles Times. The Los Angeles Times is not supposed to be a religious paper, but the editor writes: "The Bible is the one great book for all peoples and all times. In it is to be found the inspiration for all civilization and all material and spiritual advancement of individuals and nations. The time will come when the Bible will be read and studied, not only in Sunday-schools, but in all the public schools of the country. The time will come when to be unacquainted with the Bible and the wisdom it teaches will mark a man as uneducated, if not indeed unfit for his duty to himself, his family, and to society at large." This statement is undoubtedly true, at least in so far as it says that "the Bible is the one great book for all peoples and all times." The year now closing has proved this beyond a question. How utterly insufficient for such days of reality and storm and stress and crisis in individual, social, commercial and national life as these, are such shallow and vapid philosophies as Christian Science, Theosophy, New Thought, Spiritualism and all similar mixtures of bombast and hot air, but how all-sufficient is the

Divine philosophy of **God's own and only** book—the Bible.

## II. THE CERTAINTY OF THE EXISTENCE, CUNNING AND POWER OF A PERSONAL DEVIL.

The second great lesson that the year 1917 teaches is the certainty of the existence, cunning and power of a personal Devil. Belief in the existence of a personal Devil such as is pictured, not in Milton or Goethe, but in the Bible, had well-nigh died out among men, but the events of the past year can be explained only by postulating his existence. How can you account for the Kaiser and his infamous generals, Von Bissing and the rest, except by seeing the Devil back of them, just such a Devil as the Bible describes?. How can you account for the abominable utterances, not only of such demonized philosophers and political writers as Nietzsche, Treitschke, and Bernhardi, but of such hitherto highly esteemed critics, theologians and philosophers as Harnack, Deissmann and Eucken, except by discerning a very brainy, very astute Devil back of them? It is not hard to believe in a personal Devil today, indeed, it is a mark of a lack of logical acumen and candor not to believe in his existence.

## III. THAT THERE MUST BE A HELL IN THE WORLD TO COME.

The third great lesson of the year 1917 is that there must be a hell in the world to come. In recent years men have had no faith, or a very hazy faith, in there being a very dreadful hell in the world to come, but these present days demand Hell. What else can compensate for the nameless, indescribable atrocities committed by German officers of culture and intelligence upon the women and children of France and Belgium, but a hell as awful as that described in the Bible? In the light of the events of the present year, of course, there is a hell. If there were not, there would be a strange and unaccountable lack in the moral order of the universe. If I did not believe in Hell in such days as these it would be difficult for me to believe in a holy and righteous God.

## IV. THE TERRIBLE RESULTS OF THE EVOLUTIONARY HYPOTHESIS WHEN CARRIED TO ITS LOGICAL CONCLUSIONS.

The fourth important lesson of the year 1917 is the terrible results of the evolutionary hypothesis when carried to its inevitable logical conclusions. There is not time to go into that at any length, but if there were I could show you by quotations from Nietzsche, Treitschke, Bernhardi, Klaus, Wagner and other German philosophers and political writers, upon whose writings lies the immediate responsibility for the present war, that the war was the direct product of German Neo-Darwinism. For example, Friedrich Wilhelm Nietzsche, to whose philosophy more than that of any one else the German state of mind that led to this war is due, says in his book, "The Joyous Wisdom," Section 377: "We children of the future do not by any means think it desirable that the kingdom of righteousness and peace should be established on the earth. . . . We rejoice in all men who, like ourselves, love danger, war, and adventure. . . . We count ourselves among the conquerors; we ponder over the need of a new order of things, even of a new slavery—for *every strengthening and elevation of the type* 'man' also involves a new form of slavery." Of course, the whole meaning of this is that *the survival of the fittest,* Darwinian evolution in its extremist form, is a beneficial thing, and demands war as a beneficial institution. Klaus Wagner, in his book, "War," page 183, says, *"Unless we choose to shut our eyes to the necessity of evolution,* we must recognize the necessity of war. We must accept war, which *will last as long as development* and existence; we must accept eternal war." Prof. Ernst Hasse says in "Die Zukunft des Deutschen Volkstums," page 126, "'War is the father of everything,' says Heraclitus. It will be the father of the new German race of the future." This was written as long ago as 1908. The evolutionary origin of this opinion is evident to any one familiar with evolutionary teaching. General von Bernhardi says in his famous book, "Germany and the Next War," to which many attribute the present war more than to any other single writing,

"The efforts directed toward the abolition of war must not only be termed foolish, but absolutely *immoral,* and must be *stigmatized as unworthy of the human race.* . . . The weak nation is to have the same right as the powerful and vigorous nation! *The whole idea represents a presumptuous encroachment on the natural laws of development."* Heinrich Treitschke, whose teachings share with those of Bernhardi and Nietzsche the dishonor of being chiefly responsible for the present ruthless war spirit in Germany, says in his book, "Politics," Volume 1, page 121, "The Germans let the primitive Prussian tribes decide whether they should be put to the sword or thoroughly Germanized. Cruel as these processes of transformation may be, they are a blessing for humanity. *It makes for health that the nobler race should absorb the inferior* stock." Of course, such a philosophy is clearly evolutionary. No one can read the writings that created in Germany the spirit that led to this war and that inspired the methods by which this war has been carried on, without seeing that this war is the harvest of the seed that Darwin sewed when he gave to the world his theory of Evolution by Natural Selection, and that Herbert Spencer sowed when he gave to the world the phrase, "The survival of the fittest" and the philosophy that this phrase embodies. The Germans are persuaded that they are "the fittest" and therefore that the Belgians and the rest of "the inferior stock" must get out, and that it does not matter much how they are exterminated. This may seem to some of you like evolutionism gone mad, but in point of fact it is only evolutionism carried to its logical issue. It is the direct outcome of the type of philosophy that has ruled our colleges and universities, and even some of our theological seminaries, for a generation. We are talking about the necessity, for our safety's sake, of getting the German language out of our schools; it is far more necessary for our safety, and for the safety of the whole human race, that we get this soulless, cruel, remorseless philosophy of evolutionism, the egg of which was laid in England and hatched in Germany, out of our universities, colleges and high schools. Sow evolutionism as taught by

Darwin and Spencer and you reap Nietzsche, Treitschke and Bernhardi, and then you find you reap the present war, with its cruelty, its lust, its murder, its rape, its agony, its death, and almost universal dissolution and hell. It was interesting week before last to hear Prof. Shailer Matthews saying in this city that the German philosophy must go, when there is no one in all the land who has more persistently labored than he to get us to do all our theological thinking in the terms of German philosophy and German criticism. If he really means what he says, he would better retract and recall some of the stuff which he has been sowing broadcast among ministers and theological students in the past six months.

## V. THE APPALLING RESULTS OF GERMAN RATIONALISM AND DESTRUCTIVE CRITICISM.

The fifth important lesson of the year 1917 is the appalling results of German Rationalism and Destructive Criticism. This war could never have been if an increasingly numerous body of German scholars since 1833, when David Strauss gave to the world his "Leben Jesu," had not been undermining the faith of German preachers, and through them the faith of the German people in the Bible as the inerrant Word of God. If the German rulers and people had continued to believe as Luther, whose four hundredth anniversary we celebrated this year, taught them to believe, then this war never would have been. But David Strauss, Ferdinand Baur, Wellhausen Graf, Friedrich Delitzsch and the rest have done their work, and behold, the war and its shame and its agonies, its death, its destruction, turning the earth that was fast becoming a terrestrial paradise, into a terrestrial Inferno, and this same Rationalism, and this same Destructive Criticism, destructive in more senses than one, we are teaching and exploiting and supporting in our theological seminaries throughout our land today, Yale, Andover, Union, Newton, Crozier, Chicago University, and many others. Are we Americans fools? Can't we lay to heart a lesson that is written so large over the year 1917?

## VI. THE INSUFFICIENCY OF INTELLECTUAL CULTURE, SCIENCE, AND PHILOSOPHY TO REGENERATE THE INDIVIDUAL, OR BRING IN THE KINGDOM OF GOD.

The sixth great lesson of the year 1917 is the insufficiency of intellectual culture, science, and philosophy, to regenerate the individual, or bring in the kingdom of God. In recent years many preachers and churches have tried to substitute regeneration by culture and education for regeneration by the power of the Holy Spirit working through the instrumentality of the Word of God, and they have sought to bring in the kingdom by culture, science, philosophy, sociology, instead of by hastening the coming of the King. Indeed, they fancied they could dispense with the King altogether, and have the kingdom without the King's coming. The year 1917 proves the utter futility and folly of all this. Every unprejudiced scholar knows that the highest purely intellectual culture in recent years has been in Germany, that Germany is the land in which what is called science and philosophy have blossomed and born fruit as in no other land. England, Scotland and America have been selecting their brightest men and sending them to Germany to complete their education. Germany illustrates to the full what science and philosophy and purely intellectual culture can do, and behold the result! Is Germany the kingdom of God on earth? No, it is the kingdom of William, the Second, and the Devil. The leaders in Germany, university bred men, many of them university professors, are displaying the most appalling brutality, the most conscienceless lying, the most shocking inhumanity, the most astonishing disregard for the most sacred rights of women and children, the most complete moral degenercy the world has seen for centuries. Germany's *"Superman"* when he is unmasked proves to be the Devil. From this time on Americans, English or Scotch will as soon think of sending their children to a smallpox hospital as a health resort as to Germany for the development of their manhood.

## VII. THE UTTER FAILURE OF MAN WITHOUT GOD.

The seventh great lesson of the year 1917 is a lesson every year since the fall of Adam has taught, but this year with peculiar emphasis, and that is, the utter failure of man without God. For years now the doctrine that has been most popular in many circles has been the Doctrine of the Dignity and essential Deity of Man. It has not been said right out, perhaps, but it has been implied in much that has been said in poetry, novels, science, philosophy, and even theology, that man is sufficient unto himself and could get along very nicely without God. We have dropped God out of our science. We have dropped God out of our philosophy. We have dropped God out of our ethics. We have dropped God out of our statesmanship, our legislation, our education, our psychology, our sociology. Man is the whole thing. "And He that sitteth in the heavens has laughed" (Ps. 2:4) and said, "Go on without me and see where you will get." And where have we gotten? To Hell! Man has proved an utter failure. At the present time he has proved a success at nothing else but at destroying his fellowmen. "Oh, look at our inventions," we have been crying. "Look at our telegraph and telephone, by which we talk to people thousands of miles away. Look at our steam cars, by which we fly across the land. Look at our steamships, by which we fly across the water, and our aeroplanes, by which we fly through the air (and kill innocent little children at school and babes at their mothers' breasts), and our submarines, by which we fly under the water." Yes, and what is the principal use to which we see them all being put in this year of grace 1917? To kill men, women, and innocent babes. Man is an utter failure left to himself. We need God. Ignoring God, the nations of the earth have plunged into war. They are all war-weary. They all want to quit, but nobody knows how, except the Russians, and they are making the worst botch of it of all. We need God, oh, how sorely we need God, and we need the old Gospel, too, the Gospel of Christ crucified for His enemies, risen, coming again. We need not only to have it preached, but applied to life.

## VIII. THE FOLLY OF LIVING FOR THE WORLD AND WHAT THE WORLD HAS TO GIVE.

The eighth great lesson of the year 1917 is the folly of living for the world and what the world has to give. God is always crying. "If then ye be risen with Christ, seek those things which are above, where Christ is seated on the right hand of God; set your affection on things above, not on things on the earth." (Col. 3:1, 2.) But the events of the present year have been crying it out with a voice of thunder. See how thrones and governments are toppling; see how fortunes are vanishing into thin air; see how forms of governments are changing and passing; see how men are dying; see how homes are going to pieces; see how reputations are tumbling; see how vast armies are passing from the field of honor into the shades of Sheol. Oh, what folly in such days as these to live for money, honor, fame, pleasure, or anything else that belongs to this fast fading mundane sphere. "Seek the things that are above, where Christ is, seated at the right hand of God. Set your mind on the things that are above, not on the things that are upon the earth." (Col. 3:1,2.)

## IX. THE COMING OF OUR LORD JESUS DRAWETH NIGH.

The ninth great lesson of the year 1917 is, *the Coming of Our Lord Draweth Nigh*. The present state and course of things cannot go on much longer. Something new, altogether new, must happen. And to the thoughtful man the only new thing that promises any permanent solution of our grave and overwhelming perplexities and embarrassments is the long-promised coming of King Emmanuel. The times are ripe for it. Furthermore, these are just such days as God tells us will immediately precede the rising of the Morning Star, the soon rising of the Son of Righteousness with healing in His wings, the glorious coming of King Jesus. Let me read you again from the Bible God's description of the days that immediately precede the coming of the King: "But know this, that in the last days, grievous times shall come, for men shall be lovers of self, lovers of money, boastful, haughty, railers, disobedient to parents, unthankful, unholy, without natural affection, implacable, slanderers, without self-control, fierce, no lovers of good, traitors, headstrong, puffed up, lovers of pleasure rather than lovers of God; holding a form of godliness, but having denied the power thereof." (2 Tim. 3:1-6).) Now turn from that dark picture that is being fulfilled right before our eyes, and look at another that begins with great darkness, but ends in unutterable brightness and glory, Luke 21:25-28. "And there shall be signs in sun and moon and stars; and upon the earth distress of nations, in perplexity for the roaring of the sea and the billows; men fainting for fear, and for expectation of the things which are coming on the world: for the powers of the heavens shall be shaken. And then shall they see the Son of man coming in a cloud with power and great glory. *But when these things begin to come to pass,* look up, and lift up your heads; because your redemption draweth nigh."

## X. THE FOLLY OF SETTING DATES.

The tenth lesson that the year 1917 teaches is closely connected with the ninth, that the coming of our Lord draweth nigh, and should always be kept in mind in connection with that. *This tenth lesson is the folly of setting dates for the return of our Lord, or for specific events connected with His return.* Our Lord Himself has warned us in the most solemn way that we must not presume to do this. He says, "It is not for you to know times or seasons, which the Father hath set within His own authority" (Acts 1:7). The year 1917 has abounded to a hitherto unexampled degree in men who in defiance of God's Word have presumed to more than hint that Jesus would come for His Church at Pentecost this year, and when Pentecost had passed they taught that He would come at the "Feast of the Trumpets" in September. I implored one brother that he would not print what he had written on this subject, which was plainly unscriptural. Printed, however, it was, and circulated by the tens of thousands, resulting in the delaying of God's work, the wasting of God's money, the dishonoring of God's Word, and the bringing of the Blessed Hope into reproach, and now in thirty-six hours 1917 will have passed into history, the Lord is not here and Jesus Christ is saying again in a voice like the voice of many waters, "It is not for you to know times or seasons, which the Father hath set within His own authority."

## XI. WE MUST WORK THE WORKS OF GOD WHILE IT IS DAY, FOR THE NIGHT COMETH WHEN NO MAN CAN WORK.

Now we come to the eleventh and last great lesson that this year 1917 teaches to which we have time to listen this morning, *we must work the works of Him that sent Jesus Christ while it is day: the night cometh, when no man can work.* It is certain that we are fast hurrying toward the end, fast hurrying toward that dark night that shall precede the sunrise. Fast hurrying toward the night when no man can work. Fast hurrying toward the closing of the days of opportunity at home and abroad. If you have money to give, give it now. One hundred dollars now will mean more than thousands or even millions a little while from now. Are stocks down now? They will be up, up in the air, a little while from now. Have you prayers to pray? Pray them now. They won't count a little while from now. Have you souls to save? Save them now. Get to work at it at once, for the night is fast hurrying on when no man can work. Have you sins to confess? Confess them and put them away before the sun goes down tonight. Have you misunderstandings with your fellowmen to be straightened out? Up and at it, the night cometh when they will all be asleep and you cannot reach them. Listen once more to Jesus as He says again in the words of our text, "We must work the works of Him that sent me, while it is day: the night cometh, when no man can work."

# DR. TORREY'S WORKS

## STUDIES IN THE LIFE AND TEACHINGS OF OUR LORD

A consecutive, systematic course of studies in our Lord's life and teachings, divided into 140 lessons, each complete in itself, and adapted either to individual or class use. The method of the book is that of modern science; first a discovery of the facts, and then a classification of the teachings.
**Cloth $1.50**

## HOW TO WORK FOR CHRIST

An encyclopedia of all the approved methods of personal, pastoral and evangelistic work. The result of the experience of years in pastoral, evangelistic, missionary and open air work. 518 pages.
**Cloth $2.50**

## THE BIBLE AND ITS CHRIST

A book for today. Dr. Torrey's addresses to business, professional and university men. They state in a scholarly but popular way the proof that the Bible is the Word of God, and that Jesus Christ arose from the dead, and show the causes, consequences and cure of infidelity.
**Paper, 25c; cloth, 75c**

## THE PERSON AND WORK OF THE HOLY SPIRIT

A thorough study of all that the Bible has to teach about the Person and Work of the Holy Spirit as tested by personal experience. It discusses fully and frankly all the modern theories and vagaries on this important subject, and subjects them to the test of Scripture. **Cloth $1.00**

## BIOLA BOOK ROOM
**536-558 South Hope St., Los Angeles, Cal.**

# DR. TORREY'S WORKS
## (Continued)

## WHAT THE BIBLE TEACHES

The only book of its kind. All that the Bible gives on each of the great doctrines is brought together and the teaching summarized. Everything built upon a thorough study of each passage in its context. A comprehensive and thorough compendium of the teachings of the Bible. 535 pages, large 8 vo..................................................................**Cloth $2.50**

## THE RETURN OF THE LORD JESUS

A sane, systematic and thorough presentation of the teaching of the Bible regarding the Second Coming of Christ. One of the best books to put in the hands of any one beginning the study of this subject ..............................................**Paper, 30c; cloth, 60c**

## HOW TO BRING MEN TO CHRIST

A plain, simple, forceful treatise on the subject of personal work. It was Dr. Torrey's first book and has had a very large sale. Not so comprehensive as **Personal Work**..........**Paper, 15c; cloth, 75c**

## THE SHEPHERD PSALM

### By Dr. R. A. Torrey

A wonderful exposition of this famous Psalm in Dr. Torrey's masterly style............**Paper bound 25c**

---

## BIOLA BOOK ROOM
### 536-558 South Hope St., Los Angeles, Cal.

# BOOKS ON THE SIGNS OF THE TIMES

## THE VOICE OF GOD
### By Dr. R. A. Torrey
A collection of Dr. Torrey's sermons on present day subjects. His latest work. **Bound in Cloth $1.25**

## OMINOUS DAYS! OR, THE SIGNS OF THE TIMES
By E. L. Langston. Treats of Israel and the dispensations ............**Cloth 40c**

## AT HAND: THINGS WHICH MUST SHORTLY COME TO PASS
An outline of prophetic future, so interesting that once begun must almost be finished at a sitting. A masterly exposition............**Cloth 85c**

## GOD'S OATH
By Ford C. Ottman. A practical interpretation of the prophets and a study of the spiritual life of the Old and New Testaments............**Cloth $1.25**

## THE EVOLUTION OF THE KINGDOM
By William B. Riley. Dr. Riley first defines the kingdom of God and then gives a Scriptural description of it. Then follow chapters on the tribulations and the translation, the kingdom and the resurrection body, the great usurper's short reign, the Biblical order of millenial events, the kingdom of God complete "in heaven," the historical ministry of pre-millennialism, and the significant signs of the times ............**Cloth 75c**

## FUTURE EVENTS, WITH NUMEROUS PROPHETIC DETAILS
By Walter Scott. Very satisfactory answers to one hundred forty questions asked by eager inquirers, including: "Will the Lord come personally or by the spirit?" "Will the Lord's coming be pre-millennial or post-millennial?" "Will evil increase or decrease before the Lord comes?" and many others of equal interest............**Cloth 35c**

## AFTER CIVILIZATION—WHAT?
By Edward G. Rowland. Bears a message of the weightiest character, one which is of the highest importance to everyone now on earth. ............**Paper 15c**

## THE GREAT APOSTACY SET IN
By A. Sims. Showing the falling away from sound doctrine among the professed followers of Christ ............**Paper 15c**

**BIOLA BOOK ROOM**
**536-558 South Hope St., Los Angeles, Cal.**

# TITLES IN THIS SERIES

## The Evangelical Matrix
## 1875-1900

■ 1. William R. Moody
*D. L. Moody,*
New York, 1930

■ 2. Joel A. Carpenter, ed.
*The Premillennial Second Coming:*
*Two Early Champions*
New York, 1988

■ 3. - 6. Donald W. Dayton, ed.
*The Prophecy Conference Movement*
New York, 1988

■ 7. Delavan Leonard Pierson
*Arthur T. Pierson*
New York, 1912

■ 8. Helen Cadbury Alexander Dixon
*A. C. Dixon, A Romance of Preaching*
New York, 1931

■ 9. Amzi C. Dixon
*The Person and Ministry of the Holy Spirit*
Baltimore, 1890

■ 10. Arthur T. Pierson, ed.
*The Inspired Word: A Series of Papers and Addresses Delivered at the Bible Inspiration Conference,*
*Philadelphia, 1887*
London, 1888

■ 11. Moody Bible Institute Correspondence Dept. *First Course — Bible Doctrines, Instructor— R. A. Torrey; Eight Sections with Questions,*
Chicago, 1901

# The Formation of A Fundamentalist Agenda 1900-1920

■ 12. Amzi C. Dixon,
*Evangelism Old and New*,
New York, 1905

■ 13. William Bell Riley
*The Finality of the Higher Criticism; or, The Theory of Evolution and False Theology*
Minneapolis, 1909

■ 14.-17 George M. Marsden, ed.
*The Fundamentals: A Testimony to the Truth*
New York, 1988

■ 18. Joel A. Carpenter, ed.
*The Bible in Faith and Life,
as Taught by James M. Gray*
New York, 1988

■ 19. Mark A. Noll, ed.
*The Princeton Defense
of Plenary Verbal Inspiration*
New York, 1988

■ 20. *The Victorious Life:
Messages from the Summer Conferences*
Philadelphia, 1918

■ 21. Joel A. Carpenter, ed.
*Conservative Call to Arms*
New York, 1988

■ 22. *God Hath Spoken: Twenty-five Addresses
Delivered at the World Conference on
Christian Fundamentals, May 25- June 1, 1919*
Philadelphia, 1919

# Fundamentalism Versus Modernism
# 1920-1935

■ 23. Joel A. Carpenter, ed.
*The Fundamentalist -Modernist Conflict:
Opposing Views on Three Major Issues*
New York, 1988

■ 24. Joel A. Carpentar, ed.
*Modernism and Foreign Missions:
Two Fundamentalist Protests*
New York, 1988

■ 25. John Horsch
*Modern Religious Liberalism: The Destructiveness
and Irrationality of Modernist Theology*
Scottsdale, Pa., 1921

■ 26. Joel A. Carpenter,ed.
*Fundamentalist vesus Modernist
The Debates Between
John Roach Stratton and Charles Francis Potter*
New York, 1988

■ 27. Joel A. Carpenter, ed.
*William Jennings Bryan on
Orthodoxy, Modernism, and Evolution*
New York, 1988

■ 28. Edwin H. Rian
*The Presbyterian Conflict*
Grand Rapids, 1940

# Sectarian Fundamentalism 1930-1950

■ 29. Arno C. Gaebelein
*Half a Century: The Autobiography of a Servant*
New York, 1930

■ 30. Charles G. Trumball
*Prophecy's Light on Today*
New York, 1937

■ 31. Joel A. Carpenter, ed.
*Biblical Prophecy in an Apocalyptic Age:
Selected Writings of Louis S. Bauman*
New York, 1988

■ 32. Joel A. Carpenter, ed.
*Fighting Fundamentalism:
Polemical Thrusts of the 1930s and 1940s*
New York, 1988

■ 33. *Inside History of First Baptist Church, Fort
Worth, and Temple Baptist Church, Detroit:
Life Story of Dr. J. Frank Norris*
Fort Worth, 1938

■ 34. John R. Rice
*The Home — Courtship, Marriage, and Children: A
Biblical Manual of Twenty -Two Chapters
on the Christian Home.*

Wheaton, 1945

■ 35. Joel A. Carpenter, ed.
*Good Books and the Good Book: Reading Lists by
Wilbur M. Smith, Fundamentalist Bibliophile*
New York, 1988

■ 36. H. A. Ironside
*Random Reminiscences from Fifty Years of Ministry*
New York, 1939

■ 37 Joel A. Carpenter, ed.
*Sacrificial Lives: Young Martyrs
and Fundamentalist Idealism*
New York, 1988.

# Rebuilding, Regrouping, & Revival 1930-1950

■ 38. J. Elwin Wright
*The Old Fashioned Revival Hour
and the Broadcasters*
Boston, 1940

■ 39. Joel A. Carpenter, ed.
*Enterprising Fundamentalism:
Two Second-Generation Leaders*
New York, 1988

■ 40. Joel A. Carpenter, ed.
*Missionary Innovation and Expansion*
New York, 1988

■ 41. Joel A. Carpenter, ed.
*A New Evangelical Coalition: Early Documents
of the National Association of Evangelicals*
New York, 1988

■ 42. Carl McIntire
*Twentieth Century Reformation*
Collingswood, N. J., 1944

■ 43. Joel A. Carpenter, ed.
*The Youth for Christ Movement and Its Pioneers*
New York, 1988

■ 44. Joel A. Carpenter, ed.
*The Early Billy Graham:*
*Sermons and Revival Accounts*
New York, 1988

■ 45. Joel A. Carpenter, ed.
*Two Reformers of Fundamentalism:*
*Harold John Ockenga and Carl F. H. Henry*
New York, 1988

**DATE DUE**

| OC 18 '91 | | | |
|---|---|---|---|
| FE 3 '92 | | | |
| AP 12 '9 | | | |
| MY 18 '94 | | | |
| | | | |
| | | | |
| | | | |
| | | | |
| | | | |
| | | | |

BT
82
.C66
1988

30735

Conservative call to arms.

HIEBERT LIBRARY
Fresno Pacific College - M. B. Seminary
Fresno, Calif. 93702